The YELLOW DOOR *Series*
CASE SUMMARY & SKELETON ARGUMENT

EDITION ONE
Copyright © Yolanda Christian
Revised January 2018

This book is for ordinary people
who represent themselves in the
UK county court

This book is dedicated to the many people
and organizations such as the PSU,
which help the Litigant-in-Person

The PSU and other organizations
do not share my personal views within.
They are impartial organizations offering
help to those who need it

The right of Yolanda Greeba Maria Christian to be identified as the
Author of this work has been asserted in accordance with
The Copyright, Designs and Patents Act 1988

This book is sold subject to the condition that it shall not,
by way of trade or otherwise, be lent, resold, hired out, or otherwise
circulated without the author's prior consent in any form
of binding or cover or digital other than that
which it is published and without a similar condition, including
this condition, being imposed on the subsequent purchaser.

Typeset & design and author copyright © Yolanda Christian

Front cover: photograph of 5 Vaughan Road, London E15
Back cover: wall with a digital date stamp of my digital
camera used to provide evidence

This book is for the ordinary person who finds him / herself alone and without legal representation in the UK county court as CLAIMANT or DEFENDANT. The contents are based on my own experience as an ordinary person without legal representation in the county court. My experience is in relation to 1 fast track case and 1 multi-track case versus a large organization / company.

<u>Disclaimer:</u> I'm not a lawyer. I'm giving you my layman [personal] experience, knowledge and analysis in an attempt to help you. I'm not responsible for any misinterpretation by you, or for any omission or mistake I might make, or for future changes in the contact details of organizations that might help you, or for future changes in legislation or court proceedings.

I believe this book will assist you in your civil matter and it will most certainly enhance your understanding of the CASE SUMMARY and SKELETON ARGUMENT—essential documents in your legal case.

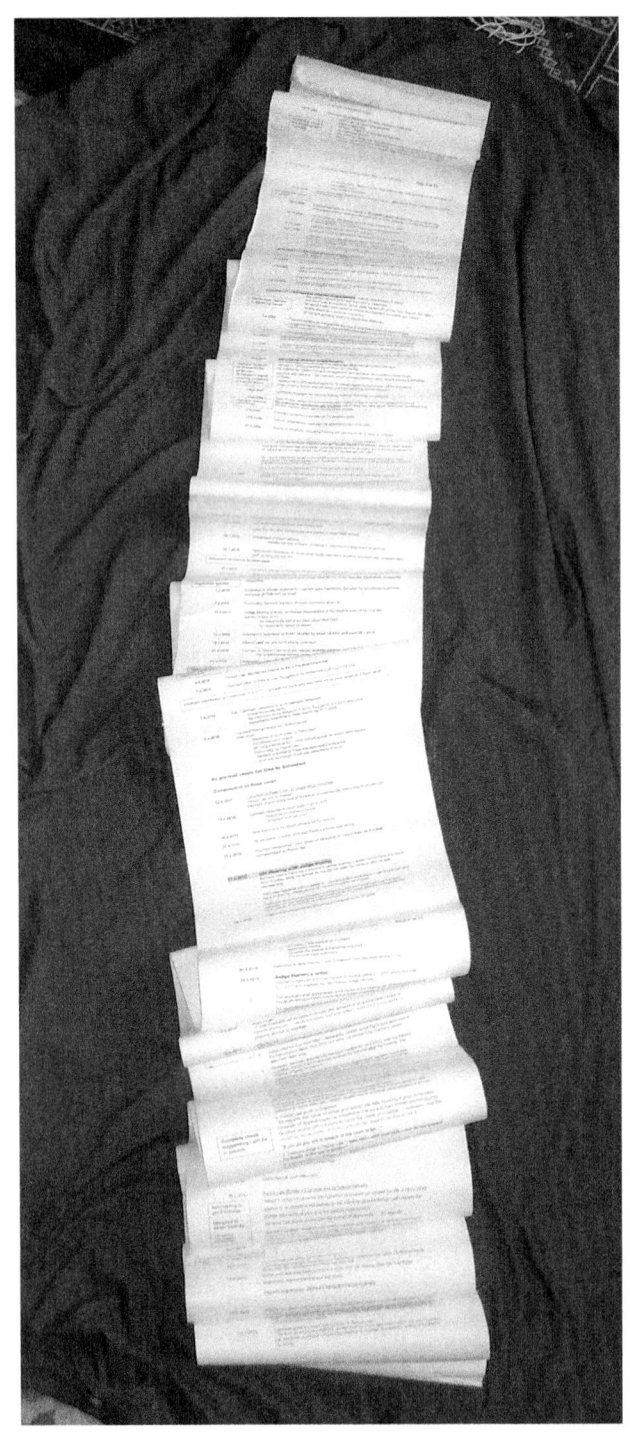

A list of filings and hearings for Case 1

Table of Contents

1. Introduction 7
2. Pro bono [free] assistance 18
   - Civil Legal Aid 18
   - The PSU [Personal Support Unit] 19
   - Pro bono solicitors at the RCJ Advice Bureau ... 27
   - Legal advice centres as part of a university ... 32
   - Bar Pro Bono Unit 33
   - LawWorks 35
   - Useful resources for the Litigant-in-Person ... 39
3. Filing & serving your documents 41
4. THE TRIAL BUNDLE 46
   - What are 'trial directions'? 47
   - The Court Order 48
5. What is a Case Summary? 50
   - CASE 1, CASE SUMMARY: Christian v Gallifordtry Partnerships Ltd ... 52
   - Trial directions, Case 1 54
   - Was CASE 1, CASE SUMMARY effective? ... 57
   - What happened in the end? 59
   - CASE 2, CASE SUMMARY: East Thames Group Ltd v Christian ... 61
   - Trial directions, Case 2 61
   - Was CASE 2, CASE SUMMARY effective? ... 64

	What happened in the end?	65
	Cross-examining the witness:	65
	Really important!	69
6.	What is a Skeleton Argument?	71
	A skeleton argument template	73
	CASE 1, SKELETON ARGUMENT: Christian v Gallifordtry Partnerships Ltd	74
	Was CASE 1, SKELETON ARGUMENT effective?	76
	What happened in the end?	77
	CASE 2, SKELETON ARGUMENT: East Thames Group Ltd v Christian	80
	Was CASE 2, SKELETON ARGUMENT effective?	84
	My original badly done SKELETON ARGUMENT	85
	Miscellaneous	107
	The final Court Order in Case 2	109
	Analysis of the Court Order	112
	What happened in the end?	116
7.	Litigants in Person (Costs & Expenses) Act 1975	119
	The awarding of legal costs	119
8.	Some conclusions & recommendations	124
9.	SUMMARY OF CONCLUSIONS	129

Introduction

CLAIMANT or DEFENDANT

Because I won my case on my own as an ordinary person without legal representation, this might inspire you in your own civil matter versus a large company or organization. However, that isn't my intention—representing yourself in the county court in a fast track or multi-track case is fraught with stress, mishap and dishonourable tactics from the other side, and could affect your health.

In Case 1, I won versus a £1.8 billion profit-making construction giant, their in-house legal team, their employed legal team based in Monument, London, and their hired barristers. In other words, I achieved the impossible.

I started out with no legal knowledge, but had strong presentational and literacy skills, a capacity for being organized, and had an excellent memory for detail. I also had vital advice from a variety of organizations as outlined in **Section 2**.

It is worth me saying to you now—you need to read the whole of this book, because there is really important information enclosed. For example, on page 69, I explain the importance of getting the names of both parties correctly entered onto documents or your legal case could be rendered invalid.

What ensued in court regarding Case 1 went on for more than 2 years [2008—2010], created a lot of anxiety and depleted my time and health. At the time, I was a professional artist collected by museums such as the Victoria & Albert Museum. I was also at a crossroad, wanted to establish a family, wanted to improve my income and needed a career-change. Unfortunately, hopes and dreams were forgotten as I became embroiled in 2 years of court hearings known as LITIGATION. OK, I won in the end; it was settled out of court for £32,000, but I must tell you that my two-year battle wasn't worth the cost to my health—most of the 'winnings' went on consequent debt, and in 2017, I have still not re-established my income or my previous robust health.

Except that JUSTICE matters.

When you represent yourself in court you're referred to as the LITIGANT-IN-PERSON [LIP]. The courts have experienced an increase in cases from the LIP due to the Jackson reforms and the virtual abolition of civil legal aid.

Please note: at the time of my litigation versus the construction giant in Case 1, I was entitled to legal aid. So why did I decide to represent myself in court?

Well . . . Solicitor **no. 1**, the details of which were found on the Law Society website, made no attempt to carry out any work for me over a long period of time yet he benefited from the legal aid fee. I made a complaint and Solicitor **no. 1** was ordered to return all legal aid costs to the Legal Services Commission and to pay me £750 for distress and delay to my claim. Unfortunately, Solicitor **no. 1** had already undermined me and caused delay to my claim. Having a solicitor behave this way towards me when I'd placed my trust in him had a negative impact on me. I have since checked the Law Society's website and see that the firm is no longer on their list. A swift 'Google' does not bring up the firm either. Who knows if they re-emerged under a different name?

I found Solicitor **no. 2** on the RCJ Advice Bureau list handed to me in their offices. Solicitor **no. 2** carried out shoddy work, was aggressive and belligerent, leaving me shaken to the core. I made a complaint and the solicitor was ordered to pay me £500. The Legal Services Commission also asked the solicitor to return all of my legal aid contributions to the amount of a further £500. However, the solicitor had already brought more delay to my claim, which diminished my sense of motivation and while I was insulted and bullied by him. Upon my notification, the RCJ Advice Bureau removed Solicitor **no. 2** from their list and retained a copy of the adjudicator's report.

I found Solicitor **no. 3** via the Internet. They were a 'posh' firm just off Fetter Lane, London EC4. I was impressed by their paralegal's attitude over the phone. However, Solicitor **no. 3** used up valuable time and made no attempt to open my important letters in their possession as we had agreed. They then declared a "conflict of interest", which meant they could no longer represent me. Meanwhile, their failure to open my letters exposed me to more distress and trespass.

"A conflict of interest"? Solicitor **no. 3** had discovered they were representing the other side as well as myself. Unfortunately, too much time had gone by to make a complaint about Solicitor **no. 3**., while I was reluctant to spend yet more time on another complaint as each one was time-consuming.

In Case 2, in which I was the DEFENDANT, my landlord's barrister told my Solicitor **no. 4** that my case was not worth defending. Solicitor **no. 4** obeyed the barrister thus ignoring relevant legislation regarding a landlord's Duty of Care. Solicitor **no. 4** was an unpleasant woman and a bully, while she knew me to be of vulnerable health.

That is why I ended up representing myself in 2 civil cases as CLAIMANT and then as DEFENDANT.

NB:
- If a legal professional recommends another professional or themselves to you, regard that with suspicion. For example, I had a local solicitor recommend a Process Server to me after explaining that he could not represent me, because he already represented my landlord. The Process Server turned out to be belligerent, refused to serve my document [to the solicitor's client!], and much later, tried to shove my front door in on behalf of my landlord. Don't be naive like me and believe in codes of conduct;

- If a friend recommends a solicitor based on their personal experience, that's of interest if you value that friend's opinion. However, this did not work out for me;

- In fact, none of the 3 solicitors in Case 1 processed my claim under the right legislation. I discovered this after a free callback from Community Legal Advice. They got me on the right track in terms of legislation. Sadly, this service no longer operates and is not to be confused with Civil Legal Advice;

- Advice from Queen Mary University's Legal Advice Centre on the Mile End Road, London gave me valuable understanding of trespass and harassment.

I litigated in Case 1 as CLAIMANT in *Christian v Gallifordtry Partnerships Ltd* from 1.8.2008 to December 2010. That's more than 2 years. The case involved:

TRESPASS,

TRESPASS TO THE LAND,

TRESPASS TO THE AIRSPACE,

DAMAGE & OCCUPATION,

INCIDENTAL DAMAGE

& PERSONAL INJURY [1]

In Case 2, I was the DEFENDANT in *East Thames Group Ltd v Christian*. My landlord knew me to have suffered trauma and personal injury caused by Gallifordtry Partnership Ltd, the construction giant. Meanwhile, I knew the landlord to be an associate of the construction giant on other building projects.

What happened was—I had not recovered from the methods employed by Gallifordtry Partnerships Ltd in Case 1 during their invasion of my Premises, nor had I recovered from their

---

[1] The date of filing on 1.8.2008 was just within the tort deadline for personal injury. Each claim has a deadline allotted to it, in which you must file your claim.

dishonourable litigation—when my landlord decided to take me to court, in order to remove the "entire roof" and the walls around me of the same Premises and while they demanded I stay living inside the ordinary house during the building works. Yes, my landlord, a housing association in east London, wanted to remove the "entire roof" above me and the walls around me and have me remain in situ. It was an extraordinary action for my landlord to bring to the county court, yet my own solicitor, **Solicitor no. 4**, deserted me.

If East Thames Group Ltd had won the right to go ahead, it would have been my worst nightmare—more intrusion during the hours of my self-employment, more exposure to potential injury, and my cat's safety would have been at risk [again]. It would have been a violation upon my person, bringing further negative impact on my health.

My problems arising in Case 2 included the solicitor of East Thames Group Ltd sending their Process Server to try and shove my front door in on 10.7.2013, days before the trial of 18.7.2013. I refer briefly to such experiences.

- *Outcome for Case 1*: It was settled out of court during mediation organized by LawWorks. I was supported by a PSU volunteer.

- *Outcome for Case 2*: The judge ordered my landlord to carry out various undertakings and did not award costs to my landlord.

I'm going to share my experiences with you. Hopefully, you will avoid some of my pitfalls and suffering, or decide not to tread the horrible path of litigation at all.

Did you know that there's no one in court to advise you? Staff can't give you legal advice, are not allowed to give it, and are not trained in this capacity. In fact, the CUSTOMER COUNTER SERVICE no longer exists to the detriment of the LITIGANT-IN-PERSON. However, PSU assistance is available for the filling in of court forms. See **Section 2**. I hope you will read this section about the pro bono [free] services available.

For purposes of clarity, CRIMINAL law is based on the principle of WITHOUT DOUBT and CIVIL law is based on 'PROBABILITY'.

CRIMINAL law	CIVIL law
WITHOUT DOUBT	PROBABILITY

When you enter the world of civil litigation as a LIP, you should feel 100 per cent wronged and have **concrete** evidence. If you have legal knowledge, you might protest about the veracity of this statement. You might say it's not true that you need **concrete** evidence, because civil law is based on 'PROBABILITY', however, if you consider what the LITIGANT-IN-PERSON is up against:

- Perhaps a large legal firm;

- Perhaps a dishonourable barrister, who has access to writing up the Court Order to your disadvantage;

- Perhaps a dishonourable barrister with access to the judge before your hearing, who will set about creating prejudice in the judge's mind about you.

A district judge may tell you that barristers "*are not allowed to lie*" and the judge may truly believe that. However, in my experience, they **do** lie. Thankfully, a circuit judge [a senior judge] may be more aware of a barrister's tricks. You will discover later that several senior judges came to my aid when I was exposed to dishonourable barristers.

Also, I once had a district judge in the county court insist I provide evidence "*beyond reasonable doubt*". I calmly informed him that he was referring to CRIMINAL law, which did not apply to my case in the county court before him.

Once you become the LITIGANT-IN-PERSON versus a large organization, you will enter a world devoid of ethics and propriety. The solicitors and barristers you face will try every trick to defeat you and land you with court COSTS.

What I refer to is the cost of court hearings: the cost of a judge's time, the cost of court administration and the cost of the other side's legal representation. In addition, there is the photocopying of the TRIAL BUNDLE, delivery of it, and other expenses such as the travel fare and cost of witnesses, etc.

If you lose and you are penniless, the court will have difficulty in extracting the costs out of you, and you should make sure that the judge and opposing side are fully aware of your lack of income, and determination to gain justice.

Solutions for the difficulties that lie in your path?

My suggestions won't automatically bring you a positive result, but I can help you make your own decisions. If you feel indignant about the situation I describe—that the LITIGANT-IN-PERSON **does not** have equal access to the law as set out in the CIVIL PROCEDURE RULES, please remember there are other countries where legal procedures are difficult to access.

I largely confine my writing to the CASE SUMMARY and SKELETON ARGUMENT and include a SKELETON ARGUMENT template, plus brief but vital advice about the TRIAL BUNDLE.

If you're the LITIGANT-IN-PERSON for the first time, you won't even know what these documents are. No one will tell you about them when you file your initial Claim or Defence either. You could go right through to a trial hearing without knowing about the existence of these documents. For example, the district judge may fail to write up in your Court Order the need for you to file these documents. This happened to me. Or the judge may assume that you're incapable of carrying out such a task, because you're the LITIGANT-IN-PERSON and he's trying to be kind. However, these documents would improve your position in every way, and it is your right to file them in the CIVIL PROCEDURE RULES [CPR].

You'll discover in Case 2 that the district judge did not comply with the CPR on my right to file a CASE SUMMARY and SKELETON ARGUMENT. However, I had them ready and waiting to file and serve and did so without hesitation.

They are not needed until several weeks or days before your trial, but if you are willing to prepare them in advance—immediately please—they will help you in the following ways:

- To focus and be grounded;

- Respond to unexpected questions from a judge;

- Argue your case as CLAIMANT or DEFENDANT;

- Prevent you from being led off track by your opponent;

- Will stand you in good stead as your opponent tries to get your case '**struck out**' [2];

- Will help quantify your claim. [How much it is worth];

- Will help quantify your legal costs. [What you might owe the court and opponent if you lose, or what you might get back for your expenditures and time if you win].

Finally, I wish somebody had given me this book years ago. For example, throughout my years of litigation, no one told me <u>I could claim</u> for my court COSTS as the LITIGANT-IN-PERSON. You won't find the information in any courthouse. I am

---

[2] '**struck out**' refers to an application by a party to get rid of the other party's case. No one can file identical applications repeatedly, but try getting court staff to respond to your complaint. I tried many times and was ignored by Bow County Court until I managed to gain the attention of Judge Hornby. He then requested that he preside over all my future hearings.

therefore pleased to include the legislation for you to claim your costs under the Litigants in Person (Costs & Expenses) Act 1975 in **Section 7**. It's near the end of the book so you have to get used to some jargon and procedure along the way. I didn't get my own costs, never mind the chance to argue about them. In both cases, my right was ignored, and I was too exhausted to pursue it.

Please note:

- Feedback on the Amazon review panel would be appreciated;

- Assist me in making any necessary amendments by contacting me on Facebook or via my blog;

- A free PDF of the Trial Bundle publication is available via Facebook;

- Let me know how you get on in your own legal matter.

Yolanda Christian

https://www.facebook.com/yolanda.christian.982

eyeofanartist.blogspot.com

2. Pro bono [free] assistance

Make sure you check the Internet for the latest details.

Civil Legal Advice (CLA)

Civil Legal Advice is a national advice line for England and Wales and is funded by legal aid. I have never used this service.

Telephone: 0845 345 4345

Minicom: 0845 609 6677

Monday to Friday, 9 a.m. to 8 p.m. Saturday, 9 a.m. to 12:30 p.m.

www.gov.uk/civil-legal-advice

You can check to see if you're eligible for free advice on the website. There is an online enquiry form or a free call back—text 'legalaid' and your name to 80010. You can get help for:

- benefit appeals;

- debt, if your home is at risk;

- special educational needs;

- housing;

- discrimination;

- help and advice if you're a victim of domestic violence;

- issues around a child being taken into care.

The PSU [Personal Support Unit]:

The PSU provides free impartial assistance. The PSU <u>cannot</u> give you legal advice. They can help you fill out court forms. They can attend your court hearing or trial as an offer of emotional support. Their London office is based at the Royal Courts of Justice. The PSU also has offices in Wandsworth, Manchester, Cardiff, Birmingham, Liverpool and Leeds. Please check the website for details about other offices in the UK.

Contact details:

The Personal Support Unit

Room M104

Royal Courts of Justice

Strand

London

WC2A 2LL

www.thepsu.org

Tel: 020 7947 7701/03 to book an appointment

Email: LondonService@thepsu.org.uk or check website

" You can find us in room M104 of the Royal Courts of Justice. This is on the first floor opposite courts 5 and 6. Court staff at reception on the ground floor will be able to point you in the right direction. Our office is open between 9.30 a.m. and 4.30 p.m. Monday to Friday. "

NB: The following is a mix of my personal experience together with some input from PSU. In a more recent revision of this book, I again approached PSU for amendments, but received no reply.

Appointments:

The banner outside the PSU office in the Royal Courts of Justice previously stated: '*The PSU can usually help you immediately*'. However, upon arrival, staff sometimes wanted to know if I'd made an appointment beforehand. I found this confusing and distressing, because I had travelled all the way there, spent money on public transport, and was then told I should have made an appointment. In addition to this, other times I phoned in advance to make an appointment and was told that no appointment was necessary—I was going full circle on this. My advice is, PSU assistance is worth having so persevere. If they cannot help you immediately, it's because they're busy supporting other litigants.

Attendance in court:

PSU can organize a volunteer to attend your court hearing. PSU will ask you for a copy of your Court Order before support can be offered. PSU volunteers are trained to provide practical and emotional support not legal guidance.

I made sure I attended hearings with a PSU volunteer. I also felt that the presence of the volunteer reduced prejudice from the judge towards me, and reduced intimidation from the other side's legal representative prior to entering the courtroom.

Having used PSU volunteers several times, I did once go to a hearing on my own, in order to take out an injunction against a landlord. Unfortunately, I'd left it too late to get a volunteer to support me. I was then treated in a heinous fashion by the district judge and left distressed and incontinent by his decision to transfer the application to Bow County Court. He refused to listen to my concerns—that there was a history of maladministration on my matters at Bow County Court. I say this resulted in the withdrawal of my application as I could not handle more stress. I was then exposed to more nuisance from the landlord and more maladministration from the courts Later, I received compensation for Kafkaesque court mal-administration thanks to the Parliamentary Ombudsman.

Filling in forms:

PSU volunteers can help you fill out forms in their office, but they can't compose the text for you. I was too late in the day to benefit from this help, however what I really valued, and which had a superb outcome for me—a volunteer would sit next to me and encourage me to open up emails and letters from the opposing side. I had grown to find this simple task impossible. I needed that support, because at the time, I suffered from Anxiety and for the life of me couldn't open correspondence. Having someone sit next to me encouraged me. There was also the comfort of a cup of tea and a chat if time allowed. In fact, thanks to a PSU volunteer cajoling me into opening up a particular envelope, I was able to bring my civil matter in Case

1 to a successful end, because the exhibit inside was a **fake**. You'll read more about this later.

'Note of hearing' and transcripts:

A PSU volunteer may also be able to take brief notes during your hearing or trial. These should act as a reminder only. PSU volunteers cannot take formal lengthy notes in court. PSU will inform you that any 'note of hearing' written by a PSU volunteer cannot be relied on for accuracy.

In my experience, PSU notes of hearing were invaluable in 2 instances, but unusable in another instance. In the latter case, I immediately applied for a TRANSCRIPT of the hearing.

I have used PSU notes at subsequent court hearings to prove that what the other party was stating at the next hearing, was not true. I did this by asking the volunteer for a copy of the PSU notes and scanned them in to be used at later moments. Mind you, if you have the money, applying for a court TRANSCRIPT of the hearing is the best way to prove what was said by a judge or the other party, although you should note that the judge is given the opportunity to approve and amend the TRANSCRIPT. That is, it may not be a 100% true TRANSCRIPT.

In addition to this, when you apply for a TRANSCRIPT, you may run into problems with busy court staff, who don't have the time to locate the relevant CD and who may tell you, *"The CD is blank"*. If you succeed in getting a functioning CD to the listed transcriber, you will then be charged for the TRANSCRIPT, which is only free if the judge has specified that you need one for an appeal and you can prove a lack of income. On top of that, the transcriber may also say to you, *"The CD is blank"*.

I found myself in this situation and was tearing my hair out. So . . . I sent an email to the transcriber stating that I was on my way to their offices to listen to the *"blank CD"*. Within minutes the TRANSCRIPT appeared in my email box. I am not joking.

A page taken from PSU notes written by a volunteer is on the next page. I originally included an explanation of the notes, but it was complex and diverted from the main aim of this book. Suffice it to say that the notes shown next page were made by a volunteer who <u>did</u> have legal training and were <u>very</u> useful. Conversely, the last note of hearing I received from another volunteer was unusable.

<u>Key to note of hearing as seen on the next page:</u>

J: district judge
YC: me
ET: the solicitor for East Thames Group Ltd

10:35.

J – I understand you want to withdraw

YC – Withdrew on 28 October

J – I've read what you've said – breakdown in communication
 – Transferred and sent it in to Central London CC.

ET – No idea until today – costs incurred
 – No indication claim withdrawn
 – email 5:00pm – no mention of withdrawal
 – surprise –

YC – Misleading info. → not approached Defendant about any legal matters

 – How could it be a defence without being served of it with documents

J – It does seem that this is the court's fault and not Miss Christian's

YC – thanks

ET – Nobody has told me – unfortunate.
 – Yesterday email received – I don't understand bundles

Phone calls:

When a [London] PSU volunteer meets a client [you] in order to support you at your court hearing or trial and the hearing is not in the Royal Courts of Justice where their office is based, the volunteer will usually call to arrange a time and place to meet you. They cannot exchange mobile numbers with you. If you need to contact the volunteer, you have to phone the PSU office.

However, I have previously received phone calls from volunteers prior to their support of my court hearing, in which they requested a face-to-face meeting with me in their office at the RCJ, that is, they were taking an interest in my case, which is very kind. My view was, 'What's the point of me travelling to the PSU office when the volunteer cannot provide legal advice and may not have legal training?' In addition to the travel expenses, they can't represent me in court; they can only hold my hand.' Also, on one occasion, I was ill in bed and the last thing I wanted was to chat on the phone or travel into central London to meet the volunteer.

My advice is, don't get into lengthy dialogue with the volunteer. If they show an interest in your case, that's great. Email them a CASE SUMMARY instead, or mention your need, such as, you'd like them to take a note of hearing, or support you in a particular way.

Later on, I was told there must be no telephone contact with the volunteer. I hope I haven't confused you. What I'm saying is—no matter how good a volunteer's intentions are, we're all human and not perfect. While a volunteer cannot and shouldn't offer legal advice or opinion or phone you for a discussion about your case, hopefully you in turn will not miss your appointment or abuse your volunteer's time and goodwill. He or she might have travelled quite a distance to support you at your hearing.

I couldn't have survived without them. They are unique.

The PSU accepts donations and is a worthy cause.

———————————————

* If you don't have a scanner, you may be able get your documents scanned in libraries and Internet cafés or use a smart phone and save to your memory stick.

Pro bono solicitors at the RCJ Advice Bureau:

The RCJ Advice Bureau provides the free legal advice of volunteer qualified solicitors. Their office is based at the Royal Courts of Justice. Please check latest details.

Contact details:
The Royal Courts of Justice
The RCJ Advice Bureau
The Strand
London WC2A 2LL
Tel: 020 3475 4373
E: admin@rcjadvice.or.uk
http://www.rcjadvice.org.uk

" Civil Law: this service can help you if you have a case in the Court of Appeal, High Court, or County Court in England and Wales, and you're not represented by a solicitor or barrister. Qualified solicitors can give you free advice, including:

- The procedural aspects of your case;

- Applications to the court;

- Referral to [free] pro bono representation;

- Referral to a free mediation service;

- Advice from a costs draftsman on costs against you. "

N.B: I wrote to the RCJ Advice Bureau regarding this book twice by recorded delivery and received no reply. Therefore, I don't have their amendments.

Appointments:

To book an appointment call 020 3475 4373 from Monday—Friday 9.30 a.m.—4 p.m. except Bank Holidays. No one is allowed more than 1 appointment per week. If you turn up without an appointment, you won't be seen.

"You can also drop in to the address from 2 p.m.—4 p.m. Monday—Friday. Our service is in great demand, so you might have to wait up to 10 days for an appointment."

In 2010, I found it difficult to get through on the phone to make an appointment. At the time, it was an 0845 number and expensive. However, I knew I had to focus on getting the solicitor's advice and persisted. In 2013, I again found it difficult and frustrating; I didn't have a landline phone and my mobile was on pay-as-you-go vouchers. I found I was spending £10 and still not getting through to speak to anyone. My sole income was then £50 per week. Telephone kiosks presented better value for money than mobile vouchers, and when I did get through, the person on the other end of the line might be unsympathetic and abrupt in nature, while I was inside a noisy smelly phone box and down to my last £1 coin.

Eventually and to my relief, I was informed that I could knock on the RCJ Advice Bureau door after 2 p.m. and would be given an appointment date verbally. This was wonderful as the cost of 2 bus journeys to knock on the door for an appointment worked out cheaper and less frustrating than using their telephone system. However, on one occasion, I knocked on the door at 4.10 p.m. and the RCJ Advice Bureau employee said he wouldn't give me an appointment as I had arrived ten minutes past 4 p.m. He didn't appear busy—he appeared to be objecting solely on the grounds of the ten minutes, while the number 25 bus had been extremely slow in the city traffic, resulting in my late arrival. I explained this and my poverty and situation and asked him did he really want me to travel in again the next day to ask for an appointment date when my income was only £50 per week. He replied, "Yes". The next day, I walked both ways from Stratford, London E15 to The Strand, London WC2 and received my appointment from the same man.

A 0207 number was then brought in, but the number has changed several times since then. A great improvement was the availability of an email address, which may have been removed. You must focus on your aim: to get an appointment for free legal advice from a solicitor.

It's important to always be polite but persistent. The service is free and is intended to help you.

Legal advice:
Pro bono solicitors have gone into the RCJ Advice Bureau at Royal Courts of Justice to provide you with free legal advice. It's invaluable professional support, but please remember that

your appointment is limited to forty-five minutes and you must turn up or cancel in good time. The appointments are in great demand from LIPs so it's essential that you're organized with your paperwork and questions otherwise you may not make good use of the allotted time.

At first, you may not know how to make use of your appointment. Also, you may get a solicitor, who doesn't operate in the area of law you need. You must take all of this in your stride. You may receive incorrect advice, because we're all human and not perfect.

What advice did I receive?
I received crucial advice on:

- the layout of documents for filing;

- the layout of a TRIAL BUNDLE, however, I struggled to understand the advice. Why not have a sample bundle available?

- what court orders and Civil Procedure Rules meant;

- what letters from the opposing side meant.

N.B: During my first session of advice at the RCJ Advice Bureau, I was given a list of legal aid solicitors to approach rather than handle the matter on my own. However, the solicitor I selected from that list, did not do any work for me. I then made a complaint as explained in my Introduction. The RCJ Advice Bureau then removed that solicitor from their list.

Be careful. I was advised by an insistent solicitor at the RCJ Advice Bureau that I must accept a 'Part 36 Offer' offered to me in Case 1, because "*you have to*". However, I had researched the matter in The White Book and did not intend to accept it. Please note, my refusal to accept the offer heightened the possibility of COSTS going against me and the solicitor was right to raise this, but she was not right to insist that I obey her instruction based on a short meeting in which she would not listen to me.

I did refuse the offer and later settled on a sum of money twice the amount of the Part 36 Offer. I must say though, if I had followed her advice I would have saved myself a lot of anguish in terms of endless court hearings and administration. However, on that day, I came away <u>without</u> the advice I needed and left fuming. Later, I came across the same solicitor and she was able to listen to my latest enquiry. To this day, I wonder if I should have followed her advice about the Part 36 Offer.

I was also advised by a RCJ Advice Bureau solicitor in Case 1—a very pleasant solicitor—on how to strike out my opponent's application, however the solicitor was not in full receipt of my information and 45 minutes is a short amount of time to exchange information and I was very tired. The result in court was—an unpleasant judge in Bow County Court, who appeared to show me immediate prejudice and who was not in possession of my court filing, dismissed my application and awarded COSTS <u>against</u> me to the amount of <u>£450</u>.

You will be pleased to know that a senior judge later removed these costs.

In the final analysis, having court orders, the legal process and a solicitor's opinion offered to me at the RCJ Advice Bureau was undeniably necessary.

Legal advice centres as part of a university

I received vital advice on legislation from the Legal Advice Centre, Queen Mary University of east London, which was written up as a letter and posted to me.

The advantage of receiving a letter is that you've got it in your hands and you can reflect on it. I was then inspired to carry out research on my own in libraries and on the Internet.

I haven't referred to legal advice centres that aren't attached to universities, because my experience of them wasn't so good. This may have been due to the demand on the legal professional from a packed room of needy individuals.

One such professional said my claim was worth £500, while it was later settled for at £32,000.

Bar Pro Bono Unit

Contact details:
48 Chancery Lane,
London,
WC2A 1JF

www.barprobono.org.uk

You can go online and see if you're eligible for a pro bono barrister. Also, the solicitor at the RCJ Advice Bureau can put you forward for a pro bono barrister.

I have experience of this service. I'm **not** recommending it to you; I'm simply making you aware of it.

One pro bono barrister provided me with an invaluable SCHEDULE OF LOSSES. If I hadn't filed it on time, my claim would have been thrown out of court and 2 years of litigation would have been wasted—I would have been crushed. The SCHEDULE OF LOSSES increased my understanding of my case.

I felt that another barrister gave me an inaccurate and pompous opinion. He referred to my cellulitis infection, [caused by the spillage of raw sewage in my garden], as "an inflammation". I didn't like that at all, because you can **die** from a cellulitis infection. There is a legal case in which a female patient contracted a cellulitis infection in hospital and it was most fortunate that her son was a barrister.

A third pro bono barrister advised me to accept the Part 36 Offer and refused to look at my evidence, which was very distressing and left me in tears.

 A fourth pro bono barrister, selected by myself, and which I regret to this day, was to help me write up PARTICULARS OF NEGLIGENCE as ordered by Judge Hornby. This barrister reduced me to a quivering wreck and also told me to accept the Part 36 Offer. He gave me an incorrect reason to support this advice. I couldn't help but feel that he was supporting the other side although it might have been that he simply wanted to bring his pro bono work to a swift end.

To my great relief, he wrote up the particulars I needed in time for the deadline. However, he refused to write in the points of law, which undermined its content. He told me this was because he didn't *know* the legislation. Make of that what you will. However, at that stage, I was able to find the points of law myself as provided on the Internet.

———————————————

LawWorks:

Contact details:

www.lawworks.org.uk

Online form: www.lawworks.org.uk/why-pro-bono/contact-us

"When asked what would have happened if they had been unable to access our services, clients of LawWorks Cymru answered, *"would have been in hospital"*, *"would be homeless"*, *"would have lost my house"* and *"would be bankrupt"*."

LawWorks is a charity working in England and Wales, which aims to connect volunteer lawyers with people in need of legal advice, who are not eligible for legal aid and cannot afford to pay. LawWorks has offices at the National Pro Bono Centre in Chancery Lane, London, and team members in Cardiff, Bristol and Manchester. I am unclear as to whether they still organize the kind of mediation I benefited from in Case 1 and which is summarized on ensuing pages.

N.B: In the revision of this book, I approached LawWorks for amendments and received no reply. A swift glimpse of their website indicates a change of staff.

As said in my Introduction, in Case 1, LawWorks brought my lengthy litigation to a successful end by organizing mediation between the construction giant and I. That is, once the paperwork was processed between the 2 parties, a firm of solicitors was brought on board to host the mediation for free, and administrate the outcome.

Prior to the awarded date of mediation, I found it traumatic dealing with the LawWork caseworker, who I experienced as condescending and shrill. She insisted I could not write up and present the 'short position' of my losses myself, treated me as inferior, and insisted that a barrister do the presentation for me. I found all of this distressing after almost 2 years of painful litigation and when she knew me to be of poor health. Consequently, the LawWork caseworker and myself went to meet the barrister. We didn't make any progress and after she had gone, the barrister, in my view, mentally assaulted me and I was left virtually suicidal.

However, on the day of mediation, I held my resolve and presented my 'short position' and losses successfully.

The selected firm of solicitors was situated in central London with beautiful offices. They provided a spacious, elegant room with a huge oval table. To the side, there was a fresh pot of coffee and nibbles. If you can imagine, I had been living on the breadline for quite some time and was probably suffering from malnutrition. Chocolate biscuits are not nutritious, but the gesture and environment were a welcome lift. I was accompanied by an experienced PSU volunteer, who provided excellent support and who I remember to this day.

I was then introduced to 2 solicitors, a man and a woman, both pleasant. They were in receipt of my 'short position' and other documents such as my CASE SUMMARY and SCHEDULE OF LOSSES. It became apparent that the woman had read through everything, but the man had not. He then began to make assumptions about my claim, which were incorrect. I think the scenario was based on 'good cop', 'bad cop'.

The man then took on the role of shuttling back and forth between the 2 parties, that is, the construction giant's employees and barrister were in the room next to me.

At one stage, the woman solicitor intervened to correct the man solicitor as to the extent of my claim, and told me that she would understand it if I wanted to refuse settlement and preferred to go to trial. Not only did she show understanding of my experience of the construction giant, but she was indicating that she would support my refusal to settle as ordered in the Court Order. This meant that if I decided to go to trial and lost, the judge would know I had good reason not to comply with the order to settle.

However, the matter *was* settled, and the barrister wrote up an agreement, which was scrutinized by the solicitors. The man solicitor then ended proceedings with an absurd, condescending comment about my claim. It was time to go. My PSU volunteer offered to buy me a sandwich . . . I went home on the number 25 bus, in theory, £32,000 richer. As with everything though, the battle was not over. When the cheque arrived, my bank suspended my account and investigated me for fraud . . . I changed banks!

In Case 2, I applied to LawWorks again for mediation with my landlord. If you remember, most of my winnings from Case 1 went on clearing credit card debt, and I wanted to be re-housed with a different landlord as I was in fear of my landlord.

Unfortunately, when I approached LawWorks, I had a similar encounter with the same caseworker. In addition to that, their manager then dismissed my application to their organization, while she knew I was in fear of my landlord and of vulnerable health. She then informed me that the landlord's own contracted mediator would offer me mediation instead. However, Common Ground refused to assist me and advised me to contact Samaritans.

If mediation with Common Ground had gone ahead, the landlord might have saved £8,500 in legal costs and £11,000 in hotel costs for the temporary re-housing of the tenant above me, plus other legal costs and other inevitable losses.

When I lodged a complaint to LawWorks chief executive officer, CBE, [Commander of the Order of the British Empire], he provided a shameful, sham response, at which point I felt the need to write to all of the Trustees.

There appears to now be a new chief executive and the LawWorks manager appears to no longer work there.

Resources for the LITIGANT-IN-PERSON:

- Are you eligible for legal aid? Try: www.gov.uk/legal-aid/eligibility. Bearing in mind what I wrote in the Introduction . . .

- advicenow.org.uk: Advicenow is an independent not-for-profit website apparently providing accurate information on rights and legal issues to the public. There is an A to Z of topics to choose from and a series of guides that take you step-by-step through issues and options. I don't have experience of this service;

- The following downloadable leaflets may be of use. They were produced for the Royal Courts of Justice Advice Bureau with funding from the Cabinet Office, Office for Civil Society Transition Fund 2011. For example, Leaflet 5 takes you through the trial process and may be useful if you are **totally** unfamiliar with the court process. Otherwise, they are overly simplistic:

Leaflet 1: Going to court - Are there alternatives?

Leaflet 2: Going to court - Before you start

Leaflet 3: Going to court - First steps

Leaflet 4: Going to court - Starting your claim

Leaflet 5: Going to court - Hearings, the trial and appeals

- www.bailii.org provides free access to finished legal cases, one of them might support your own case. You may need to experiment with the words you enter into the website's search engine. If you do find an existing case, which supports yours, then you're in a stronger position and can quote from it. For example, *Ferguson v British Gas Trading Ltd [2009] EWCA Civ 46* was a landmark case on how companies can be responsible for the harassment of the individual consumer even if the failures were created by different staff in different departments. Therefore, if your case consisted of the same elements then you would cite the case title and reference to support your own case, and quote the applicable <u>points of law</u> that were used;

- Google can throw up interesting cases too. You may need to experiment with the words you enter into the search engine;

- The White Book: You should be able to find one in any county court or at the RCJ Advice Bureau or the PSU offices. I found it difficult to use, but when I persevered, I seemed to have find what I was looking for;

- Google the Civil Procedure Rules. However, this will not give you the additional notes or known cases as in The White Book, and which barristers rely on;

3. Filing & serving your documents

| **Filing** is when you post, email or hand-deliver your document to the county court | **Serving** is when you post, email or hand-deliver your document to the other party |

Previously, you went to the CUSTOMER COUNTER SERVICE to file your document and get it stamped at the same time. However, this service has been removed.

As you can't get your copies stamped anymore, filing is now open to hidden dangers for the LITIGANT-IN-PERSON. For example, you may have filed a document by a given deadline, but when the court hearing takes place, the judge may say that he is not in receipt of it. Then the opposing side's representative may tell the judge they weren't served a copy either. The judge may then conclude you are dishonest, because you cannot show him a stamped copy of what you filed.

This is what you need to do:
You need 3 copies of everything. 1 for you, 1 for the opposing side, and 1 for the court: 'CLAIMANT copy', 'DEFENDANT copy' or 'Court copy'. You should also save all of your digital files in a methodical manner to USB memory stick, or to an email folder, or your computer desktop.

Hand-delivery:

If you hand-deliver your paperwork to file in court, you do <u>not</u> come away with proof of its delivery, because you can't get your copy stamped or watch the staff log it onto their computer system. All you can do is post it in the court postbox.

Email:

If you file by email not all county courts use an automated message of receipt. However, unlike hand-delivery, you <u>do</u> have proof of filing, because you have the original email in your Sent box. If the outgoing email comes back as rejected, then you do not have proof of filing and need to use the post.

Apparently, some courts refuse to print off voluminous emails, but they don't tell you that. Thus, the postal service becomes a more attractive option.

What if they don't acknowledge your email? They probably won't. I will explain how to prove that your email was sent and then you will be prepared.

Post:

If you file or serve by post, you can't prove that it reached its destination unless you sent it by recorded or special delivery. After that, wait a couple of days and check www.royalmail.com by entering in the tracking code on your Post Office receipt. If this shows that your post has been received and signed for, download the evidence and print it off. Keep this print out with you for the next court hearing. If the judge or opposing side says they aren't in receipt of the said document, wave the tracking receipt and your proof of purchase under the judge's nose. Not literally, of course!

It would be unusual for your tracked post not to reach its destination. If this happens, at least you will know and can claim a small amount of compensation and provide proof of non-delivery if you missed a filing deadline.

OK, you can prove receipt of post, but you can't necessarily prove the content of the envelope you served. I'll explain how to overcome this problem shortly.

Serving documents to the other side is fraught with danger because they may say they did <u>not</u> receive it, or the barrister may say he / she did <u>not</u> receive it. The best thing to do is have an <u>index of enclosures</u> on the cover page of your main document. A scan of such follows next page. Notice the table of documents. See the other side's date stamp representing receipt. [I hand-delivered to the reception desk.]

By having the stamp and index on the same page, you are proving that the recipient received <u>all</u> of the documents.

It might interest you to know there was an effort by my landlord's in-house legal team to prevent me from getting my SKELETON ARGUMENT stamped by the receptionist. A member of staff told the receptionist, in front of me, that I was "*a lawyer, not a tenant*". However, I was not a lawyer and I was their tenant. I held my ground, got my stamp and kept the original.

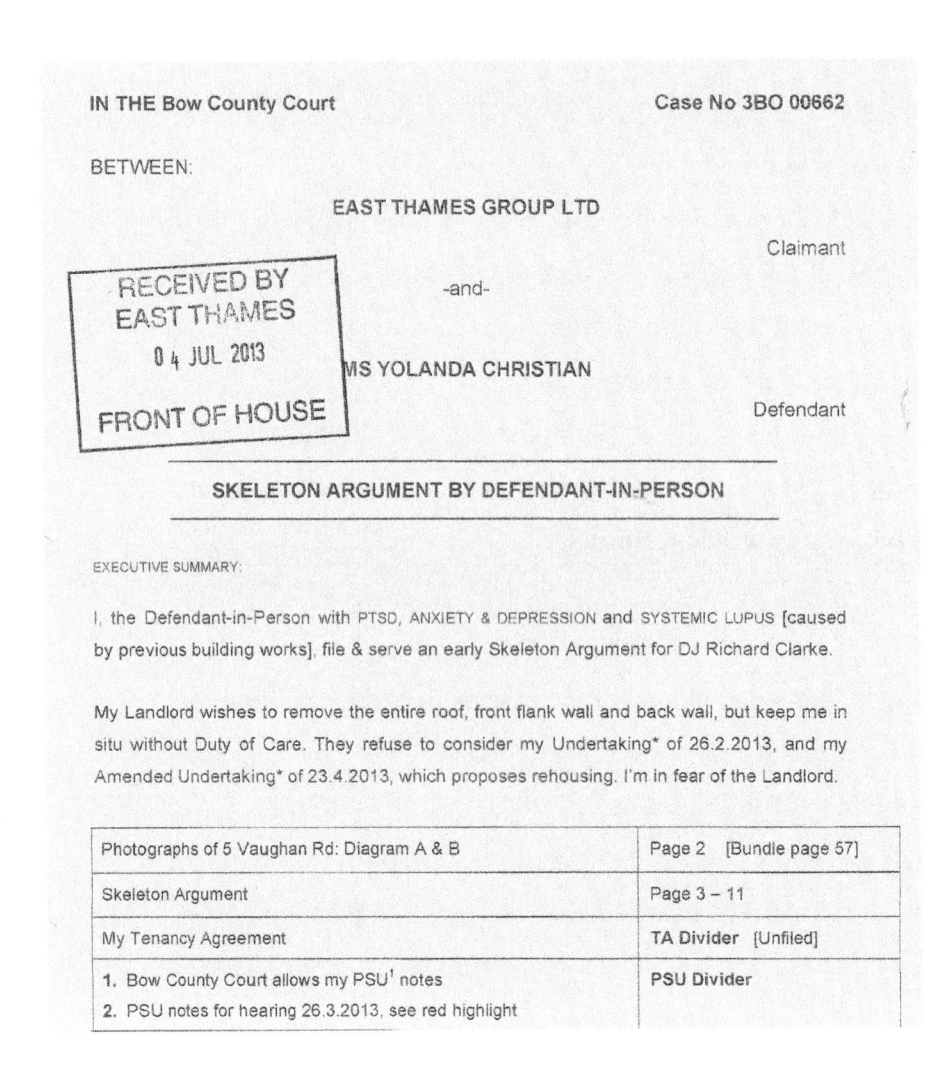

> IN THE Bow County Court
>
> Case No 3BO 00662
>
> BETWEEN:
>
> **EAST THAMES GROUP LTD**
>
> Claimant
>
> -and-
>
> **MS YOLANDA CHRISTIAN**
>
> Defendant
>
> *[Stamp: RECEIVED BY EAST THAMES 04 JUL 2013 FRONT OF HOUSE]*
>
> ---
> **SKELETON ARGUMENT BY DEFENDANT-IN-PERSON**
> ---
>
> EXECUTIVE SUMMARY:
>
> I, the Defendant-in-Person with PTSD, ANXIETY & DEPRESSION and SYSTEMIC LUPUS [caused by previous building works], file & serve an early Skeleton Argument for DJ Richard Clarke.
>
> My Landlord wishes to remove the entire roof, front flank wall and back wall, but keep me in situ without Duty of Care. They refuse to consider my Undertaking* of 26.2.2013, and my Amended Undertaking* of 23.4.2013, which proposes rehousing. I'm in fear of the Landlord.
>
> | | |
> |---|---|
> | Photographs of 5 Vaughan Rd: Diagram A & B | Page 2 [Bundle page 57] |
> | Skeleton Argument | Page 3 – 11 |
> | My Tenancy Agreement | TA Divider [Unfiled] |
> | 1. Bow County Court allows my PSU[1] notes
2. PSU notes for hearing 26.3.2013, see red highlight | PSU Divider |

If hand-delivery isn't possible, email your document[s] to the opposing side as a PDF file, but <u>copy-and-paste the index</u> of page 1 within the email, so that it can be seen in the Sent email box at a glance. You can then provide proof of serving and its contents by making a screen dump of your Sent email to show the judge. I'll explain how to do this shortly.

Screen dumping an email:

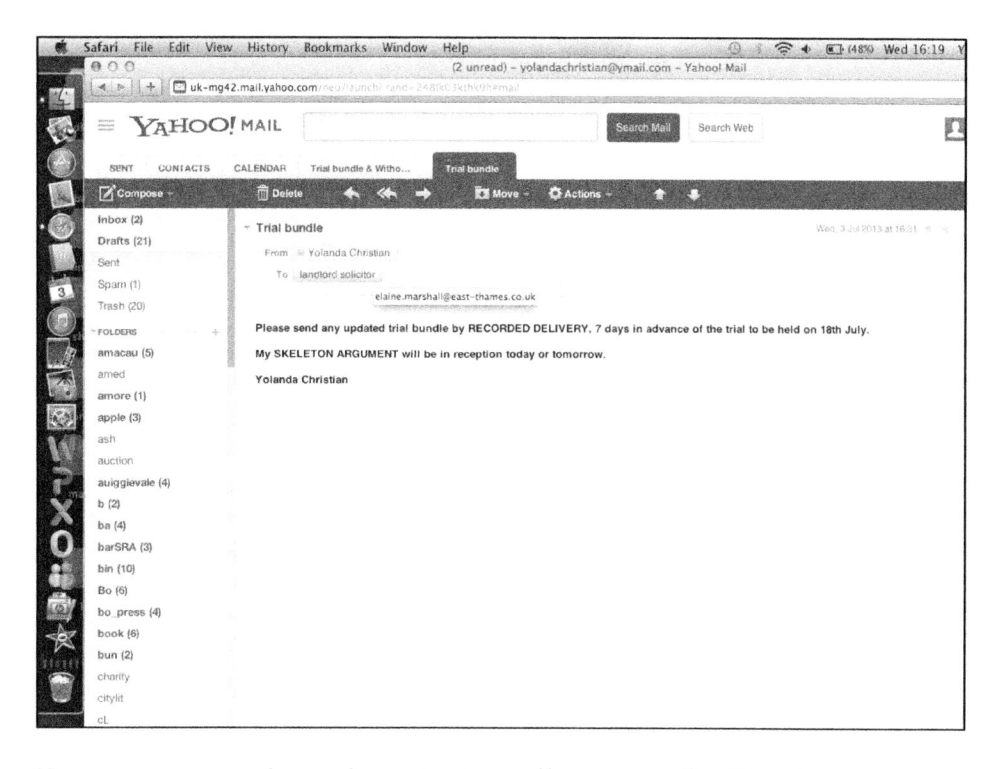

You can screen dump important emails as proof of having 'served' your document. What I mean is—on any computer there is a facility to take a snapshot, which you can then save as a jpeg or PDF file. Open up the Sent email and . . .

| On a PC, put one finger on the Control key and one finger on F13, press down, then open up Word and go: File / New / Menu / Edit / Paste / Save with a logical file name. | On my Macbook Pro, I go fingers all at the same time: Shift key / Control key / 3. A snapshot is left on my desktop, which I then save. |

4. THE TRIAL BUNDLE

A TRIAL BUNDLE is a selection of copied documents representing both parties. The bundle is for the judge and both parties to use at a trial. A bundle may also be available for any witness. The bundle consists of 1 or more lever arch files with the documents in a set order.

The compilation of the TRIAL BUNDLE is the right of the CLAIMANT as set out in the Civil Procedure Rules. The CLAIMANT copies the TRIAL BUNDLE three times over—for the court, for the opposing side and for him / herself.

The TRIAL BUNDLE should be the result of an <u>agreement</u> between both parties. Unfortunately, I have never experienced such an opportunity. I have only ever experienced sabotage.

The judge should notify both parties about the filing and serving of the TRIAL BUNDLE in his Court Order. Unfortunately, if you are the DEFENDANT it doesn't necessarily mean you will receive your copy of the bundle from the CLAIMANT, as the other party may wish to undermine you and deprive you of your right to defend yourself, which is of course <u>unacceptable</u>.

I write in greater detail about the TRIAL BUNDLE in a separate publication. However, I have a crucial point to make right now—my landlord's in-house legal representative did everything possible to deprive me of a copy of the TRIAL BUNDLE as was my entitlement. They claimed to have left it in my front garden. Of course, it wasn't there. I had a small front garden, consisting of a bay window, 2 waste bins and 2 recycling bins. The judge had to give me his copy, and upon my subsequent inspection, it was clear that my landlord's in-house legal representative had removed pages of my witness statement and carried out other sabotage, such as photocopying my high-resolution photographs so badly that no one could understand the images.

In such a situation, you need to list all disgraceful acts and file an '*Urgent Letter to the Judge: SUBMISSIONS ON THE TRIAL BUNDLE*'. On the day of your trial, and before the trial begins, ask the court usher to hand a copy of this same letter to the judge as it may not have reached the judge via court staff. On entering the courtroom and after the judge has introduced him / herself, stand up and ask if you may make SUBMISSIONS ON THE TRIAL BUNDLE. Present the sabotage to your documents, which will contribute to the other side losing their COSTS.

What are trial directions?
I didn't have a clue about legal jargon or legal process, but eventually I began to see there was a logic involved.

After a first hearing, a judge reaches a decision on how the court matter should proceed, usually after both sides have presented their argument during the hearing. A judge may then *direct* it towards a trial date. More likely, he / she will *direct* it towards another hearing following the need of additional documents, say, a medical report is required, or the lodging of an expert witness is required, or perhaps the other side has provided a point of law as to why the case should be 'struck out' and you need to respond. Deadlines for filing and serving may be in the Court Order. This is what is meant by 'trial direction'.

The trial directions are usually verbalized in front of you at the end of the hearing. It's wise to make a note of them, or if you have a PSU volunteer at your side, he / she may take notes for you, although you shouldn't rely on the notes for accuracy.

You need to be alert. Emotionally, you will be winding down at the end of the hearing, but this is when you need to concentrate the most as the judge may mention something you don't understand, and you'll have missed your opportunity to ask for an explanation. Also, if you don't have notes of the judge's verbal decision, the other side may take advantage of this and introduce an error into the Court Order to cause mayhem. In addition to this, a judge may accidentally give directions that undermine your rights within the CPR.

Please refer to the trial directions presented after the 2 CASE SUMMARY examples provided later on in this book.

The Court Order:

The trial directions will be typed up into a Court Order, which is done by the clerk, however:

– When the Court Order arrives in the post check it for inaccuracies. Compare it to what was said in court. Do this by consulting your note of hearing and memory;

- The clerk may have made a mistake in the wording;

- The wording may have been interfered with by the opposing side's barrister to undermine you. No, the barrister is not allowed to do that;

- You might think an error on the Order can do you no harm, but in my experience, it's there quite deliberately and will cause you trouble further down the line if you don't tackle it;

- I have received incorrectly worded Court Orders that have gone on to give me problems and extra work, while the very last Court Order in Case 2 was given by the district judge to the barrister to write up. The barrister then used ambiguous wording and created omissions;

- If you think there's an error in the Order, seek advice and write an *Urgent Letter to the Judge*. This should be as brief as possible and have a copy of the Court Order stapled to it.

The Court Order will be posted to you. Don't rely on that. In my experience, after I made complaints about Bow County Court administration, I stopped receiving court post and my court file would be absent for my court hearings. I then made it my habit to enquire at the court counter about any outstanding post, [which was still in service at the time], and to have a spare file with me for the judge.

    Exhausted yet?

5. What is a Case Summary?

Thankfully, the title explains the purpose of this document, whereas the title of other documents often left me baffled. For example, what is a STATEMENT OF ISSUES or a SCHEDULE OF LOSS?

For the CASE SUMMARY:

- You are to summarize your case as CLAIMANT or DEFENDANT and confine it usually to one A4 page;

- You end the CASE SUMMARY with a STATEMENT OF TRUTH and add your signature and date;

- You should use numbered paragraph spacing for each point and use a size 12 font.

The problem is—if you're distressed, ill, are being harassed, or if the case is complex, or if you don't like writing, or your English isn't that good, or maybe you're just not confident—how do you write one up? I'm afraid it's a case of drafting and redrafting until the important facts remain. It takes time.

I do feel that if you have no understanding of the law, but you're willing to use your common sense and list the facts logically and chronologically with dates and times, then you will be close to having a CASE SUMMARY.

For CASE 1, CASE SUMMARY, I kept re-examining my text for ambiguity and error and amended it accordingly. I also reduced the amount of words to comply with the set word limitation given in the Court Order. I worked on the text on and off over a period of time, giving myself time to think over the words and their meaning.

Each time, ask yourself—Is it an accurate summary? Is it beyond rebuke? Is it a straightforward read? Does it need a diagram?

Don't forget, you might be able to get pro bono legal advice on this, but I have a feeling that in the first instance it's crucial for you to spend time drafting it yourself, because no person is going to care about your case as much as you do.

CASE 1, CASE SUMMARY is on the next page.

CASE 1, CASE SUMMARY: *Christian v Gallifordtry Partnerships Ltd*

IN THE CENTRAL LONDON COUNTY COURT   Claim No. 8BO 03293 / 8BO 03295

BETWEEN:

MS YOLANDA CHRISTIAN

Claimant

- and -

GALLIFORD TRY PARTNERSHIPS LIMITED

Defendant

CASE SUMMARY

1. I, Yolanda Christian, am the Litigant-in-Person and Assured Tenant of East Thames Housing Group Ltd at 5 Vaughan Rd, London E15 4AA;

2. On 28 February 2005, the Defendant, a construction giant, took possession of 2 Faraday Road, London E15 and demolition work began. However, planning permission was not given to the owner of the site, *Toynbee Housing Association*, until 14 June 2005. The site was adjacent to no. 1, 3 and 5 Vaughan Road and separated by a continuous shared party wall between the three neighbours;

3. The Defendant intended to rebuild the party wall. No. 1 & no. 3 Vaughan Road received a Party Wall Award, however, I did not at No 5, nor did I receive any Notice as set out in The Party Wall etc Act 1996;

4. On 5.7.2005 pre-11.00 a.m. I received a threatening phone call from *Sprunt* demanding immediate access to my Premises. At 11.15 a.m., *Sprunt* faxed me a 5-page 'Method Statement', which held the Defendant's logo;

5. At 14.57 p.m., the Defendant's contract manager replied to my faxed complaint: "...*we are extremely disappointed to hear that no one from East Thames Housing has been in touch with you to explain what in fact has been agreed...*"

6. However, on 5.7.2005, the Defendant did then enter my Premises for more than a year of trespass, trespass to the land, trespass to the airspace, damage and occupation and personal injury.

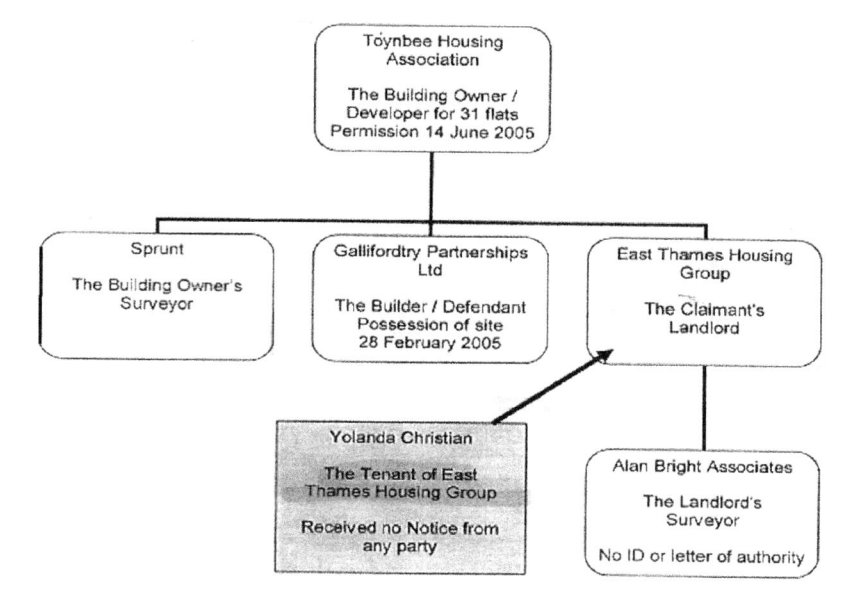

```
                    ┌─────────────────────────┐
                    │  Toynbee Housing        │
                    │  Association            │
                    │                         │
                    │  The Building Owner /   │
                    │  Developer for 31 flats │
                    │  Permission 14 June 2005│
                    └─────────────────────────┘
                              │
        ┌─────────────────────┼─────────────────────┐
        │                     │                     │
┌───────────────┐  ┌─────────────────────┐  ┌───────────────────┐
│    Sprunt     │  │ Gallifordtry        │  │ East Thames       │
│               │  │ Partnerships Ltd    │  │ Housing Group     │
│ The Building  │  │                     │  │                   │
│ Owner's       │  │ The Builder /       │  │ The Claimant's    │
│ Surveyor      │  │ Defendant           │  │ Landlord          │
│               │  │ Possession of site  │  │                   │
│               │  │ 28 February 2005    │  │                   │
└───────────────┘  └─────────────────────┘  └───────────────────┘
                             │                       ▲
                    ┌─────────────────────┐          │
                    │ Yolanda Christian   │──────────┘
                    │                     │
                    │ The Tenant of East  │  ┌─────────────────────┐
                    │ Thames Housing Group│  │ Alan Bright         │
                    │                     │  │ Associates          │
                    │ Received no Notice  │  │                     │
                    │ from any party      │  │ The Landlord's      │
                    └─────────────────────┘  │ Surveyor            │
                                             │                     │
                                             │ No ID or letter of  │
                                             │ authority           │
                                             └─────────────────────┘
```

STATEMENT OF TRUTH

I, the Claimant, Yolanda Christian, believe that the facts stated in this document are true.

Signed: *Yolanda Christian*

Dated: 10 Oct 2010

As my matter involved several parties, I included the diagram. [Don't be afraid to use your initiative . . .] You see, I didn't want the opposing representative to argue that Gallifordtry Partnerships Ltd was <u>not</u> the right DEFENDANT. At first glance, you see, the DEFENDANT would be Toynbee Housing, the owner of the build. However, the construction giant's method statement bore their logo and this was in my view evidence that they had used their own initiative and were not ordered by Toynbee to trespass.

Don't forget your Statement of Truth, signature and date.

Trial directions for Case 1:

After numerous hearings with different judges, District Judge Dixon ordered a Fast Track trial for my case.

Fast Track is for claims estimated to fall within the £15,000 to £25,000 range. In other words, he elevated my claim, which had originally been filed as a set of small claims due to incorrect advice given to me by the Legal Services Commission.

The Court Order stated:

9) Not more than seven nor less than three clear working days before the trial, the <u>Defendant</u> shall file at court an indexed and paginated bundle of documents * which complies with Rule 39.5 of the Civil Procedure Rules and the practice direction thereto, and shall serve a copy of it on the <u>Defendant</u>. The parties shall endeavour to agree the contents of the bundle before it is filed. The bundle shall also include:

a) <u>a case summary of not more than 250 words;</u>
b) <u>a statement of the issues to be decided by the court</u>;
c) <u>a skeleton argument of all parties</u>

* The Order doesn't use the words 'TRIAL BUNDLE' so you might not know what is being referring to. Hopefully, you will have checked the CPR online.

Referring to the above underlined words, the Court Order writes that the '<u>DEFENDANT</u>' is to file the trial bundle, when that is the CLAIMANT's right. It was my right to file it as set out in the CPR. So, what happened? Here are some possibilities:

- The DEFENDANT's barrister may have deliberately written the word 'DEFENDANT' on the Order to usurp my entitlement to produce the trial bundle;

- The judge may have assumed that I, as the LITIGANT-IN-PERSON, was incapable of producing a trial bundle and he was trying to help me out;

- The court clerk may have made a mistake;

- The court clerk may have been invited to make the mistake by the opposing side's barrister.

At the time, I had no idea how to produce a trial bundle, or that it was my right as CLAIMANT to produce it. The information isn't available in the county court. However, it <u>was</u> my right and the Court Order deprived me of that right.

You would think the courts would provide a leaflet, wouldn't you? That is why I wrote the publication: '**Trial Bundle**'.

What then happened was that the law firm on behalf of the 'DEFENDANT' took advantage of the 'mistake' in the Court Order by producing the trial bundle themselves.

Their bundle consisted of voluminous pages of misleading and 'vexatious' material, which a humble LITIGANT-IN-PERSON wouldn't understand, although I did notice that the construction giant's barrister had lifted a sample case from The White Book, which implied—to me anyway—that he was 'winging' it.

When I received my copy of the DEFENDANT's bundle by courier, it did have the desired effect on me—it filled me with fear. I was baffled. I couldn't read it.

I am grateful to the judge for his perspicacity on this matter. His Honour, Judge Hornby, angrily asked the barrister on that day: "*What exactly do you call this?*" and held the bundle up in disgust. The barrister did not reply, and I note that he did not represent the construction giant again—another dubious barrister took his place!

My case was then upgraded, for a second time, by Judge Hornby to multi-track—worth £25,000+ and with no fixed limit. He considered it too time-consuming for a Fast Track trial. He said it would take him too long to read my filings and that it should be transferred to Central London County Court.

I asked Judge Hornby for permission to increase the wordage of my CASE SUMMARY. This was granted.

Exhausted yet?

Was CASE 1, CASE SUMMARY effective?

I was completely ignorant about all legal matters and did not prepare the CASE SUMMARY until I was ordered to do so, which was almost 2 years after I filed my original batch of small claims [which I was subsequently ordered to consolidate].

It's much better to work on it straightaway. If you've forgotten why, re-read the Introduction!

The CASE SUMMARY *was* effective:

1. It honed matters in my head. If only I had produced it at the start of my litigation instead of having to verbally repeat my claim to a variety of judges—two years of litigation might have been reduced to one;

2. During hearings, judges would ask me questions out-of-the-blue. If I had prepared a CASE SUMMARY, I could have referred to it or simply handed it to the judge. This would have saved time, distress, and or an inability to speak due to stage-fright on the day;

3. When I finally served my CASE SUMMARY, it showed the construction giant that I was not incapable, and they were set to lose their COSTS, which were mounting as Gallifordtry Partnerships Ltd had then hired the services of a major law firm based in Monument, London and had changed barristers;

4. The CASE SUMMARY shows the court you're not a time-waster. If you hand it to the judge at the first hearing, you're cutting down on prejudice and impressing him / her;

5. During the very last hearing, I was at the end of my tether and couldn't have endured more. My CASE SUMMARY had an <u>immediate</u> impact on the judge, plus the news from me that the construction giant's main exhibit was a **fake**.

    The judge then gave a direction for the DEFENDANT to settle out of court and ordered them to disclose documents that they had repeatedly refused to disclose to me despite the CPR on DISCLOSURE OF DOCUMENTS.

<u>N.B:</u>

During my very last hearing in Case 1, my court filings were not available for the judge to read, that is, they were lost in Central London County Court by accident, or on purpose, despite my hand-delivery to the then existing Customer Counter Service. I believe this difficulty arose, because I was conducting a complaint against Bow County Court. Fortunately, by that stage, I had developed a habit of taking a <u>spare</u> copy of my filings with me. I was then able to hand one to the judge, who refused to offer a copy to the barrister! Nice!

What happened in the end?

Case 1 was transferred from Bow County Court to Central London County Court, because the presiding judge did not have time to read my ridiculous, voluminous files at Bow County Court, and because the case was upgraded to multi-track. The judge had just suffered the death of his wife. I was in awe of his composure and it is a measure of the man that he would say 'Good morning' if we passed each other on the Romford Road.

When my case file was transferred—unknown to me—Rose Court contacted the new judge prior to what was to be the final hearing. They informed the judge of my concerns:

- That the DEFENDANT had repeatedly denied me DISCLOSURE OF DOCUMENTS and Bow County Court would not act;

- That the DEFENDANT had made repeat attempts to strike out my claim with duplicitous applications and Bow County Court would not act.

I was able to show the new judge emails from the construction giant's barrister's own chambers—which showed that the barrister had done his best to usurp my trial directions while I was having a **toilet break** during a previous court hearing! I also had new evidence, which showed that the DEFENDANT's main defence document was a **FAKE**. So, when the judge asked me about my unsuccessful and lengthy pursuance of the DEFENDANT's lack of disclosure:

"Ms Christian, are you not concerned about the existence of a Party Wall Award?"

I was able to reply . . . and it was a truly delicious moment:

"No, your Honour, the document's a fake."

This was the last straw for the judge, who became angry with the barrister and said:

"Mr —, you are getting right UP my nose."

He then ordered both parties to attempt to settle the matter out of court and it *was* eventually settled for £32,000.

Ah, remember . . . if the PSU volunteer in the PSU office had not helped me open up and read vital post from the DEFENDANT, one of which contained the fake exhibit, then I would never have been able to bring my matter to an end!

Don't get too excited about the money I settled on— the bulk went on credit card debt and on recovery, and afterwards for a long time I was too ill to enjoy my success anyway! That is the reality. I didn't make the best use of the 'winnings' either. Maybe I should have used them to generate more income rather than paying off all of my debts in one go?

Lastly, during that last hearing when I became upset it was amazing to have a PSU volunteer reach out and hold my hand.

CASE 2, CASE SUMMARY: *East Thames Group Ltd v Christian*

Trial directions:

The district judge wrote on the Court Order:

4. Pre-trial Checklists dispensed with.

The direction meant more unequal access to the law for me:

1. '*Pre-trial Checklists dispensed with*' means there will be no DISCLOSURE OF DOCUMENTS before the trial bundle is made. The judge may have done this to speed things up, but it deprives a party from requesting important documents from the other side;

2. In Case 1, pre-trial checklists were not dispensed with, yet the construction giant repeatedly failed to provide DISCLOSURE OF DOCUMENTS. And refused to agree on the simultaneous exchange of witnesses by email, which probably meant they didn't have any!

3. **With the Checklist dispensed with, there was no mention in the Court Order about a CASE SUMMARY or SKELETON ARGUMENT. I filed and served them anyway;**

4. At a CASE CONFERENCE MEETING to discuss the trial of Case 2—I was not provided with a copy of the TRIAL BUNDLE from the CLAIMANT. When I protested, the judge saw me as a vexatious litigant, which was intimidating. However, due to my polite persistence, he gave me *his* copy and extended the time allocation of the trial to half a day so that I *would be heard*;

CASE 2, CASE SUMMARY: *East Thames Group Ltd v Christian*

IN THE CENTRAL LONDON COUNTY COURT   Claim no. 8BO 00662

BETWEEN: EAST THAMES GROUP LTD   <u>Claimant</u>
– and –
MS YOLANDA CHRISTIAN   <u>Defendant</u>

CASE SUMMARY

1. I am Yolanda Christian, Assured Tenant of **East Thames Housing Group Ltd**, not **East Thames Group.** I live at 5 Vaughan Rd, ground floor flat, with sole use of the garden. 5a is the upstairs flat;

2. Essential works relate to Newham Council's Dangerous Structure Notice to repair the flank wall above the front doors of 5 and 5a within 24 hours on 30.9.2011. However, my landlord demolished my garden wall instead on 7.10.2011 causing me much distress;

3. On <u>**8.2.2013**</u>, Jennifer Marius, the Landlord's area manager, emailed me about 'essential works to 5a Vaughan Rd';

4. On 11.2.2013, the upstairs tenant was rehoused, but I was not. I was asked to provide access for 8 weeks to builders, which was without regard for my self-employment, vulnerable health, or Quiet Enjoyment. I emailed Ms Marius for more information as my tenancy agreement allows on page 12, RIGHT TO INFORMATION [7], but she did not respond;

5. On 14.2.2013, I emailed Ms Marius attachments: Exhibits A, B, C, and Exhibit F [the Council's Notice], while on 19.2.2013, I emailed her Exhibit G, re: symptoms akin to Systemic Lupus;

6. On 25.2.2013, Ms Marius emailed me about temporary rehousing, however the temporary rehousing would not house my elderly cat as well;

8. On 4.3.2013, Ms Marius' emailed her intentions to: *"remove the entire roof, take down the parapet wall on the flank elevation and back addition... the brick parapet walls to be removed down to the plumb line"*. However, I was to remain inside the ordinary house;

[Statement of Truth and signature]

[I've used 254 words, which would fit on 1 page]

Was CASE 2, CASE SUMMARY effective?

1. I believe the district judge did not read it, because the CLAIMANT did not put it in the trial bundle. I don't believe that the barrister read it either. This may be because the barrister's client advised the barrister not to read it. The purpose of instructing in this way, would be to eliminate any possible fear the barrister might have about losing their client's case, or to prevent the barrister from forming a sympathy for me;

2. I believe that my social landlord's in-house solicitor contrived not to file my CASE SUMMARY in the bundle. That is, it was not in the bundle for the trial among other omissions and sabotage. I was then able to provide copy on the day, but the judge did not set aside time to read it;

3. However, the DEFENDANTs exclusions and sabotage of the bundle would have a negative impact on the judge's opinion of my landlord and how costs be awarded;

4. Yes, my CASE SUMMARY was effective, because it helped me to focus, which ultimately resulted in the other side losing all of their legal costs, more than £8,000 for the barrister, plus solicitor costs, plus other costs, amounting to about £20K;

5. If the barrister for the other side does not produce a CASE SUMMARY then all the better for you. You will appear to be more professional.

_____

What happened in the end?

I brought the sabotage of the trial bundle to the attention of the district judge in the opening minutes of the trial under 'SUBMISSIONS ON THE TRIAL BUNDLE':

1. I did this by urging the court usher to hand in my one-page letter, *'Urgent Letter to the Judge'*, just before my trial was to begin;

2. As soon as the trial began, I stood up and asked the judge to consider my SUBMISSIONS ON THE TRIAL BUNDLE. I had prepared what to say in advance by rehearsing in front of a mirror!

3. I had already filed on this scandalous matter, but received no acknowledgement from Bow County Court, therefore I had no alternative but to stick my neck out, which was nerve-wracking;

4. I write in greater detail in my publication: 'Trial Bundle'.

Cross-examining the witness:

I cross-examined the witness and loved every minute of it. Watch out, you're the LITIGANT-IN-PERSON and the judge may assume you're incapable of carrying out this task and deny you this right—or the other side may try to usurp you by creating some kind of diversion.

When it was my turn to cross-examine the landlord, one of my first questions to my landlord's area manager and witness, Jennifer Marius, was: *"Have we ever met or spoken before these court proceedings?*" The judge gasped with disapproval as Jennifer Marius struggled to reply, because you would have expected some contact between us before any expensive court proceedings were initiated.

I further explicitly proved during my cross-examination of the Witness that Jennifer Marius had offered me temporary accommodation on 25.2.2013 for building works to take place on my Premises, while she had also filed for injunctive proceedings on the same day. That's pretty damning stuff from which there is no way back. Unfortunately, it would be confusing if I were to explain more about my tactics in court that day and what I might or might not reveal until the big day.

In addition, my landlord had denied me Right to Information as set out in my tenancy agreement and had not given me a *reasonable* amount of time to make an informed decision. Even worse, Jennifer Marius had made no attempt to provide me with a decant policy as was my legal right. Inappropriate to say the least.

Originally, I had complained by email to Jennifer Marius about their forthcoming and dangerous building works and had then eventually been offered a hotel room with en suite facilities so that the building works could take place. However, I couldn't accept this as the hotel would not accept my cat, while my landlord offered to put my cat into a cattery for 8 weeks or more. I knew my cat would not be able to cope with that because:

1. He was old with thyroid disease, kidney disease and arthritis, and being put into a cattery long-term would have left me unable to administer his medicines and caused him great distress;

2. He'd spent the last 15 years, since a kitten, by my side and had an outdoor spirit. I knew that incarceration in a cattery would finish him off;

3. More importantly, it was never going to be 8 weeks of building works as set out in the landlord's draft. Historically, their repairmen had made a roof leak repair last for more than 2 years. However, my own hired roofer dealt with the 2-year problem in <u>45 minutes</u> by unblocking the bottom of the drainpipe. The water had been backing up and pouring out at the top onto the outside wall and causing dampness within my flat. Prior to my hiring a roofer, I had endured a succession of the landlord's workmen. Some were pleasant or unpleasant, insulting, or just stupid. I also endured the landlord's customer advocate standing in my hallway and smiling with pleasure as he reduced me to tears.
   The point is: if the landlord was capable of taking 2 years to sort out a simple leak, then my cat could have ended up in a cattery for 2 years or more. He never would have survived;

4. I found legislation on the RSPCA website to support my cat: The Animal Welfare Act 2006, Section 9.

As a consequence of me successfully objecting to the landlord's application, my cat got to 'enjoy' life until 5.9.2015; that's when the moment arrived and I had to have him put to sleep. My cat had been my companion for 17 years. I still miss him. But thanks to my determination, he got to have 2.5 more years of living at my side, while my landlord had wanted to condemn him to incarceration and ultimately death.

Ironically, while my court battle in 2013 was fought to preserve his life and mine, and my later relocation to another landlord meant that I was safe from East Thames Group Ltd, in fact, cats suffer from extreme stress when moved to unfamiliar territory. In his new 'safe' home, he began to deteriorate before my very eyes and went from good physical agility to staggering about on sore limbs, lost weight, became skeletal, was prone to falling over, maintained a healthy appetite, but was too afraid to use the new garden. In his last days, he developed an aggressive tumour in his jaw.

I despise the landlord for unnecessary stress placed on him and myself. Their actions affected us deeply. All East Thames Group Ltd had to do was behave in keeping with our tenancy agreement. I would not be *still* struggling with my health. I have been experimenting with supplements such as Vitamin D for aches and pains and immense fatigue. My current symptoms are hair-loss and after 10 years of left-side facial pain there remains muscle tissue loss, which has affected my good looks! I have not recaptured my income.

Really important!

You may have noticed in CASE 2, CASE SUMMARY that the CLAIMANTs title was 'East Thames Housing Group Ltd', but everywhere else I refer to them as 'East Thames Group Ltd'. In fact, the landlord filed under numerous names, and I draw your attention to this or it could affect your success:

1. A CLAIMANT or DEFENDANT's <u>name</u> needs to be written on the paperwork correctly. For example, if you win your case against the DEFENDANT yet their name is incorrect, then your successful outcome will be invalid;

2. Check company names on www.companieshouse.gov.uk

3. In both Case 1 and 2, there were discrepancies about the name of the other party. For example, in my ignorance, in Case 1, I filed the construction giant as *Gallifordtry Partnerships <u>Plc</u>*, whereas the correct name was *Gallifordtry Partnerships <u>Ltd</u>*. I could have lost my claim by continuing with this error, while the construction giant failed to correct me;

4. In Case 2, my landlord regularly filed under a variety of names, which appeared at a glance to be correct, so watch out for this.

In other words: make sure you get the names for both you and the other side right—down to the last letter and use of punctuation.

This is how I used to attend court hearings . . . obsessed . . . and totally ignorant of the law

6. What is a Skeleton Argument?

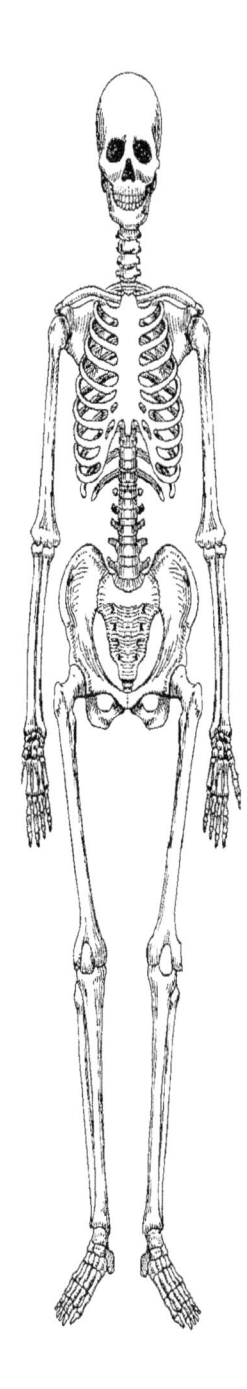

The SKELETON ARGUMENT is precious. It might be the <u>first</u> time a trial judge is acquainted with the case. Also, it's the one time where the other side cannot <u>tamper</u> with the contents.

It's a written summary of your legal argument that you file and serve no less than 3 days before your trial.

It's the bare bones of your case in terms of fact and legislation.

| If it's short, the judge will read it. |

I've already explained to you in the Introduction why it's advantageous to produce a SKELETON ARGUMENT as soon as possible. Right at the start, please. It won't be easy, but you will thank me later and it will extend your knowledge and understanding.

You will undoubtedly rework it as time goes by. It will be impossible to get it 'right' straight off, but with advice given to you and your own research, you will be heading in the right direction.

The CPR provisions are CPR PD 52A and CPR PD 52C.

The order of information for your SKELETON ARGUMENT is:

– Case background;

– Points of Law;

– Submission of Fact;

– Summary;

– Relevant reading of selected documents in the bundle, past cases to support your case.

You'll be pleased to know, thanks to the Internet, there's a template for a SKELETON ARGUMENT in this book. You should be able to find it on the Internet or copy what's on the next page.

The Court of Appeal has focused on the length of the SKELETON ARGUMENT. It should be as brief as possible—3 pages, plus copies of relevant legislation tagged on at the back.

In *Midgulf v Groupe Chimique Tunisien [2010] EWCA Civ 66*, Lord Justice Toulson stated that there is a *"tendency to burden the court with documents of grossly disproportionate quantity and length"* in reference to the SKELETON ARGUMENT. As well as inviting rebuke or a cost sanction, or having the SKELETON ARGUMENT disallowed by the judge, you risk not having it read by the judge due to sheer lack of time.

A SKELETON ARGUMENT template

IN THE   Case No
BETWEEN:

                    [Name]   Applicant
                    -and-
                    [Name]   Respondent

[Applicant]
SKELETON ARGUMENT

A. Nature of Case/Background

1)

2)

B. Points of Law

1)

2)

C. Submissions of Fact

1)

2)

Summary

Skeleton Argument prepared by [name], the Litigant-in-Person

Dated this   day of   20xx

Reading List

1) Documents to be read, pagination refs from the bundle…
2) Relevant legal cases to support your case

CASE 1, SKELETON ARGUMENT: *Christian v Gallifordtry Partnerships Ltd*

IN THE   Case No

BETWEEN:

[Name]   Applicant

-and-

[Name]   Respondent

[Applicant]

SKELETON ARGUMENT

A. Nature of Case / Background

1) I am the Litigant-in-Person and of vulnerable health. The Defendant entered my Premises on 5th of July 2005 until 21st of August 2006 without any Party Wall Award as required of The Party Wall etc Act 1996. What then followed was Trespass, Trespass to the Land, Trespass to the Airspace, Damage and Occupation and Personal Injury.

B. Points of Law

1) **The Party Wall etc Act 1996, Section 20, Interpretations (b)** states that I am the "adjoining owner" with the same rights as a property owner and that I was entitled to all notice, rights and compensation as laid out in the act. [Copy of legislation at back of this argument]

2) **Party Structure Notices Section 3, (1)** states that as adjoining owner I am entitled to specific notice. [Copy of legislation at back of this argument]

3). The law on Negligence applies as I suffered avoidable and foreseeable personal injury and losses as set out in my SCHEDULE OF LOSSES.

C. Submissions of Fact

1) I am in receipt of a longstanding Assured Tenancy Agreement and therefore I am the "adjoining owner".

2) The DEFENDANT's exhibit of a Party Wall Award is a FAKE. [trial bundle pagination ref]

3) My medical report refers to a serious cellulitis infection caused by the flooding of raw sewage into my garden, contracted via eczema in my bare feet as I went into the garden to hang out my washing. During the year-long trespass, I developed an irregular heartbeat, high blood pressure and anxiety, which then developed into PTSD.

4) The DEFENDANT has repeatedly failed to disclose documents to me.

Summary

I am a peaceful long term Assured Tenant and cultivated a beautiful garden and I needed normal enjoyment of my Premises in order to conduct my self-employment as an artist and digital designer. This right was destroyed by the Defendant, an £1.8 billion profit-making company, who filed and served a FAKE Party Wall Award, and acted in a negligent manner and caused the collapse of a public sewer in the vicinity of my garden etc.

Skeleton Argument prepared by [name], the Litigant-in-Person

Dated this   day of   xx

Reading List

1) At the time, I did not understand what this meant. I did not supply any reading list or legal cases to support my case.

Was CASE 1, SKELETON ARGUMENT effective?

In Case 1, I wasn't directed to file a SKELETON ARGUMENT. When I first filed my original batch of small claims on 1.8.2008, I didn't have a clue about legal matters and lurched from one baffling situation to another. If only I'd prepared the argument in advance with the aid of legal advisers. Instead, I produced a thick messy wad of pages in a tiny font size that no judge in their right mind would want to read and I actually *expected* this to win me an Appeal!

In fact, the leap in knowledge was too great for any LIP at that stage. It's only now I can provide you with a good example of what my SKELETON ARGUMENT *could* have been.

The example given is confined to 3 pages. Note the use of "I" and "my" instead of CLAIMANT to personalise my status and emphasise the David & Goliath situation. If you're of vulnerable health, say so in the Submission of Fact. If my SKELETON ARGUMENT had been prepared, I might have shortened 2 years of litigation and saved myself a year.

I hope you will benefit from this. If I'm ever in court again, I know I will.

N.B.

Early on, Community Legal Aid sent me a guidebook on The Party Wall Act, however in court matters, you need to refer to **the actual** legislation and points of law as found on the Internet.

What happened in the end?

How was I supposed to know the points of law contained in the SKELETON ARGUMENT you've just read?

Thankfully, Queen Mary, University of east London pointed me quite early on to the law on TRESPASS and HARASSMENT. I then read about TRESPASS TO THE LAND, TRESPASS TO THE AIRSPACE, and other forms of trespass in my local library, but I had very little confidence in using the information. And one windy rainy day, I received a phone call from Community Legal Aid, which directed me towards THE PARTY WALL etc ACT 1996. In addition to that, a district judge alerted me to the point of law at Section 20 of the Act. After that, an Information Officer at RICS gave me an overall understanding of the Act.

I need to tell you something special about the then Information Officer at RICS. He was *the* man; the only person, who explained everything to me, yet he was unsighted. I have since carried out voluntary work at RNIB.

Just prior to my Appeal hearing in July 2010, the opposing side's barrister discussed with the judge in private that NUISANCE and PERSONAL INJURY could not sit together as had been previously ordered by a district judge. I don't know if that's true or not, but the judge listened and then struck out NUISANCE. I was baffled as usual. However, the canny senior judge still found in my favour at the Appeal hearing . . .

It was a terrible time—the judge had us in and out of court all day. Fortunately—penniless as I was—I had prepared a flask of coffee, a sandwich and had a Kitkat at the ready. When you feel utterly usurped and alone in the world, these things are a welcome luxury.

So we were in and out of court. Inevitably, both parties needed a toilet break while being heard. The barrister utilised my toilet break to give the judge an unfiled document, which ignored his client's lack of disclosure and which ignored my pending expert witness etc. When it was the barrister's turn to relieve himself, I mentioned the discrepancies to the judge [after having scrambled to read the document on the hoof] and while his young protégées in miniskirts squirmed on the benches behind me.

Judge Hornby then ordered that I proceed on NEGLIGENCE, not NUISANCE, and I was to file 'PARTICULARS OF NEGLIGENCE'. While this new deadline filled me with dread, in fact, the judge had added more weight to my claim as NEGLIGENCE is a serious matter.

For NEGLIGENCE to proceed, I had to show a loss and Judge Hornby asked me if I could do this. All I could utter at the time, was that I had a receipt for garden furniture that the construction giant had broken. In reality, my losses were far greater, but when you're ill and ignorant of the law, you can misrepresent the extent of your own losses. Please bear this in mind.

OK, the judge had heard I could prove <u>some losses no matter how small</u> and my Appeal was upheld. This meant that the barrister lost his client's application to strike out my case.

Later, a pro bono barrister's SCHEDULE OF LOSS provided me with an excellent account and which also advanced my legal knowledge and understanding on how to quantify losses.

I am so lucky that His Honour, Judge Hornby, was not repelled by the endless list of ridiculous legislation I provided in a tiny font size.

My next problem was how to write up the PARTICULARS OF NEGLIGENCE . . . and would I meet the next deadline?

CASE 2, SKELETON ARGUMENT: *East Thames Group Ltd v Christian*

Foreword:

You're allowed to file 2 SKELETON ARGUMENTs for your Claim or Defence. No more than that.

I filed my first one in advance to show my opponent that I knew what I was doing. As it happens [!] I was over-confident and exposed my naivety to the landlord well in advance of the trial. My landlord was then able to adjust their argument as necessary. Please bear this in mind.

I filed my second argument three days before the trial, because my knowledge of the law had changed. If you think about it, you could use the second one to your advantage. You could also use it to highlight sabotage of the trial bundle if you have suffered this.

My landlord filed only 1 SKELETON ARGUMENT three days before the trial, which is the norm. What wasn't normal was how the landlord's PROCESS SERVER served it . . . There was a loud knock at my front door followed by someone trying to look through my letterbox and breathing menacingly into the door. The man shoved his body forcefully against the door in an attempt to make it burst open. Thankfully, it held. He stayed there for some moments breathing heavily—I was quaking in the hallway. I heard a car door slam. My immediate reaction was to grab my coat and run out into the street, however, I realized he would be in his car parked in front of my front door. I went into the garden and peered over the wall.

The PROCESS SERVER was in his car for a good while. I tiptoed back in and opened up the 'hand-delivery'. It contained the landlord's SKELETON ARGUMENT. I decided not to read it; if my points of law were correct, it wouldn't matter what the other side said in their argument.

The filing of your SKELETON ARGUMENT is your last chance to right the wrongs and exclusions created by the other side's dishonourable tactics. That's how I used my SKELETON ARGUMENT in Case 2 as seen on the ensuing pages.

However, my original was awful. I have made up a better version for this book and you should assume it took a lot of gestation and amendment, while I ask you to write yours up straightaway.

My original badly done version appears after it, because it still has some value in terms of analysis and the judge's reaction on the day, and how very difficult it is to be the LIP.

CASE 2, SKELETON ARGUMENT, greatly revised for this book

IN THE　　　　　　　　　**Case No**
BETWEEN:

　　　　　　　　　　　　　　　　　　　　　　　　Applicant

　　　　　　　　　　　-and-

　　　　　　　　　　　　　　　　　　　　　　　　Respondent

SKELETON ARGUMENT

A. Nature of Case/Background

1) I am the landlord's Assured Tenant of 5 Vaughan Road since April 2000 and of vulnerable health. I am also the Litigant-in-Person as my landlord's barrister informed my solicitor that my position could not be defended.

2) The Claimant, my landlord, emailed me on [date] about required access to carry out building works [to the entire roof and exterior walls] of my Premises. What then followed were emails, in which my landlord ignored his Duty of Care towards me, ignored my right to a decant policy, ignored my vulnerable health and ignored the welfare of my elderly cat.

3) A visual on page x shows the DANGEROUS STRUCTURE above me, which was reported by me on x to the landlord. My landlord responded by demolishing the wrong wall, my garden wall, and has not rebuilt it.

B. Points of Law

1) The Landlord, East Thames Group Ltd, owes me a Duty of Care as their long term Assured Tenant under **The Defective Premises Act 1972: 4. Landlord's duty of care in virtue of obligation or right to repair premises demised (1)** [copy of legislation at back of argument]

2) My Assured Tenancy agreement page 12, RIGHT TO INFORMATION [7] [copy of legislation at back of argument]

3). My Tenancy Agreement also states: **Temporary Vacation of Premises (16) (16) (a)** [copy of legislation at back of argument]

4). The Animal Welfare Act 2006, Section 9.

C. Submissions of Fact

1) I have never been provided with a Decant Policy.

2) The landlord ignored my *Draft Undertaking* written up by a solicitor and filed and served on [date]. The landlord has filed it in the trial bundle as their own.

3) The landlord works will **not** take 8 weeks but may take 2 years. This is based on my previous experience . . . [evidence filed at back]

Summary

I am a peaceful long-term Assured Tenant. My medical report is supplied. The landlord wishes to remove the roof and walls around me, incapacitate me and incarcerate my elderly cat. NB: on 10.7.2013, the landlord sent a "heavy" to my home, who tried to shove my front door in.

Skeleton Argument prepared by [name], the Litigant-in-Person
Dated this   day of   xx

Reading List

1) A list of all the documents referred to in this argument and referenced against the pagination of the trial bundle.

ADD VISUALS FROM PAGE 90

Was CASE 2, SKELETON ARGUMENT effective?

The revised SKELETON ARGUMENT does a good job of presenting my case, but as you know, it has been written in retrospect.

I was still able to use my very bad original:

- as a guide when it was my chance to defend myself;

- when I cross-examined the witness;

- when I summarized at the end of my trial;

- it steadied my nerves;

- helped me when interrupted by the judge;

- helped me when the barrister exclaimed: *"Oh, do we really need to listen to this?"*

- helped me when the judge asked me to slow down and repeat myself;

Although the original version shown further on is convoluted, at times, the judge *did* listen, and I was able to hold my ground when the judge didn't want to listen. Besides, the barrister had tried to stop me from referring to my SKELETON ARGUMENT so I must have been doing something right!

My original badly done SKELETON ARGUMENT

What follows is my <u>real</u> filed second SKELETON ARGUMENT. It's longwinded and complex, which could have gone against me. This is the danger to the LITIGANT-IN-PERSON.

However, some detail may be of value in terms of expanding your way of thinking and noting the judge's reaction on the day.

I have crossed out sections of it, which may demonstrate how to be critical of your own developing argument. One of the main problems I had with the original is that I just didn't have the capacity or knowledge to edit down the main issues. I hope you can somehow take that on board.

I went beyond 3 pages, because my landlord's legal representative had filed a dishonourable trial bundle, which required referencing. I *had to* provide additional information. This was summarized under the title 'Executive Summary'; helpful advice from a RCJ solicitor.

<u>N.B:</u>

Most pages of the original and ensuing SKELETON ARGUMENT are followed by some analysis, which is then followed by the district judge's reaction to me on the day.

Page 1 of CASE 2, SKELETON ARGUMENT, the original, badly done

Please note the Tabs 1, 2, 3 and 4, which I refer to in ensuing pages.

IN THE Bow County Court   Case No 3BO 00662

BETWEEN:

EAST THAMES GROUP LTD

Claimant

-and-

MS YOLANDA CHRISTIAN

Defendant

2ND SKELETON ARGUMENT BY DEFENDANT: TRIAL 18.7.2013

EXECUTIVE SUMMARY

I, the Defendant-in-Person with PTSD, ANXIETY & SYSTEMIC LUPUS file & serve a 2ND SKELETON ARGUMENT 3 days before the trial of 18.7.2013.

I **cannot guarantee my page refs** as the CLAIMANT'S TRIAL BUNDLE handed to me by DJ Murch on 13.6.2013 — he gave me his copy — is a dishonourable bundle. The Landlord has continued to behave this way, and sent a "heavy" to my home on 10.7.2013.

My Landlord wishes to remove the entire roof, front flank wall and back wall, but keep me in situ without Duty of Care. They refuse to consider my Draft Undertaking* for rehousing of 26.3.2013, & my Amended Undertaking* of 23.4.2013. I am in fear of the Landlord.

Skeleton Argument	Page 2 – 11
My Tenancy Agreement -- not filed upfront by Claimant	Tab 1
a. Bow County Court allows my PSU[1] notes b. PSU notes for hearing 26.3.2013, see red highlight c. My Draft Undertaking* as referred to in the PSU notes [On 13.6.2013, Page 4 was <u>dishonourably filed as the Claimant's own</u> in their Trial Bundle at Page 48] d. My Amended Undertaking* filed & served on 23.4.2013	Tab 2 c. See page 4 & 5 of 10 of my document, <u>not</u> filed by the Claimant in Trial Bundle d. See last page within Tab 3
My additions to Trial Bundle filed & served on 14.6.2013	Tab 3
Previous Landlord Roof Reports	Tab 4

---

[1] Personal Support Unit, Royal Courts of justice

Comment on Page 1:

TAB 1: The landlord's barrister, together with the landlord's area manager and witness, erroneously said during our first court hearing that I was "<u>not</u> *entitled to temporary accommodation during the building works*". The landlord then filed my tenancy agreement near the back of their trial bundle and reduced the photocopying in size to make it undesirable reading. I considered the tenancy agreement to be a pivotal document that should have been at the front of the bundle. To compensate, I filed the <u>relevant</u> part of the tenancy agreement behind TAB 1;

TAB 2: The court had <u>refused</u> my request to allow me to purchase a court transcript of the first hearing at my own expense, in which I could refer to the above. Therefore, I included PSU notes of the hearing, which you can see referenced on the index page.

I was also highlighting a different matter—that I had previously produced, in court, a document called an *Undertaking*, while my landlord's solicitor went on to file it in the bundle as the *own* document. I believe their motive was to try to avoid being landed with court costs;

TAB 3: As my landlord's solicitor did not respond to the CPR regarding my entitlement to contribute documents to the trial bundle, and set out to photocopy other of my documents so badly that they were unreadable—I compensated for this by filing appropriate copies behind TAB 3;

TAB 4: As my landlord's injunctive proceedings were for the repair of the "*entire roof, flank wall*" and "*back addition*" to be done in "*8 weeks*", I provided evidence that a blocked drainpipe repair had been repaired at my own cost by my own contractor in 45 minutes, following my landlord's repairmen unsuccessful 2 years of invasive appointments.

Page 2 of CASE 2, SKELETON ARGUMENT, the original, badly done
I have removed some text, which is too personal.

	Dramatis personae:
Mrs Bennett, Hardwicke Chambers	Barrister representing my Social Landlord
Me: Yolanda Christian	I am the Assured Tenant of East Thames Housing Group Ltd living alone at 5 Vaughan Rd, E15 4AA, ground floor, sole access to garden / back of house. ~~Aged 55+ years with personal injuries as a consequence of previous building works. Self-employed outside the home. No next of kin. Have elderly pet cat~~
MEDIATOR COMMONGROUND	Contracted to the Claimant, my Social Landlord, they refused my request for mediation and suggested I call Samaritans
Mrs Christine Connelly	Upstairs tenant of 5A Vaughan Rd, aged 65+. Once worked for my Landlord as a cleaner. Has a part-time partner aged 45+, who
The Landlord's building	2 self-contained flats in one corner house with an outstanding Dangerous Structure since 30.9.2011 – DIAGRAM A -- part of the Landlord's current building proposal
Gallifordtry Partnerships Ltd	£1.8 billion profit-making construction giant, & associate of my Landlord, who entered my garden in a year of trespass, damage & personal injury to me, while my Landlord turned a blind eye
MEDIATOR LAWWORKS	Pro bono mediator, Chancery Lane. I tried throughout 2012 to get a mediation day with my Landlord to be rehoused
Jennifer Marius	My Landlord's Area Manager
Elaine Marshall, Landlord In-house Solicitor	

Comment on Page 2:

1. The Dramatis Personae was intended to assist the judge in 'who is who' in my legal case, and to take the opportunity to highlight other impropriety. You wouldn't normally include such a page unless it was a criminal case;

2. The Dramatis Personae highlighted that the landlord interfered with my NHS provision, [which I have blocked out];

3. My landlord's barrister wasn't married. When the judge asked her if she was during their little chat at the start of our case conference meeting [in which I was completely ignored], she fluttered her eyelashes and said, "*Yes*". I thus decided to pronounce her as married in all subsequent paperwork and during all court dialogue. That's how petty I was;

4. I'd exclude this page now.

———————————————

Judge's reaction Page 2:

1. The judge was concerned that 'Common Ground' had refused to mediate upon my request. Excellent;

2. I stated in my Dramatis Personae, and verbally too, that I was an <u>Assured Tenant,</u> however, in my purchased transcript of the final Judgment, the district judge had demoted me to a "<u>shorthold</u>" tenancy. Or did someone make an edit on her behalf?

———————————————

Page 3 of CASE 2, SKELETON ARGUMENT, the original, badly done
I could have simplified the visuals below …

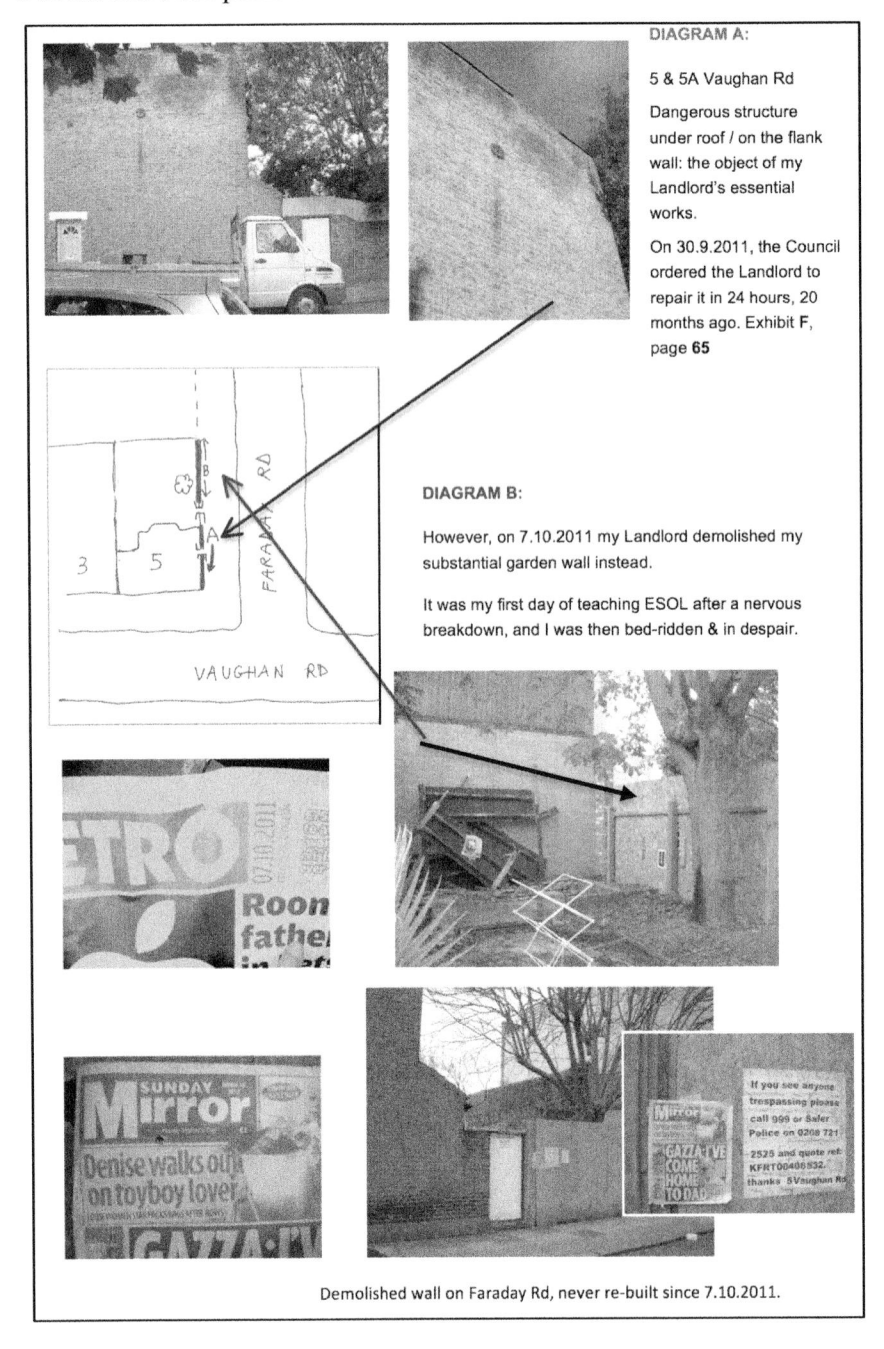

DIAGRAM A:

5 & 5A Vaughan Rd

Dangerous structure under roof / on the flank wall: the object of my Landlord's essential works.

On 30.9.2011, the Council ordered the Landlord to repair it in 24 hours, 20 months ago. Exhibit **F**, page **65**

DIAGRAM B:

However, on 7.10.2011 my Landlord demolished my substantial garden wall instead.

It was my first day of teaching ESOL after a nervous breakdown, and I was then bed-ridden & in despair.

Demolished wall on Faraday Rd, never re-built since 7.10.2011.

Comment on Page 3:

1. How would a judge know what a 'flank' wall is or where the Dangerous Structure is? The photos made the issue more real to the judge.

    a) The photos show the DANGEROUS STRUCTURE above my door and under the roof, which the Council ordered repair of on 30.9.2011 within 24 hours. Also shown on the front cover of this book;

    b) However, on 7.10.2011, my landlord demolished my garden wall instead;

    c) As the DEFENDANT, I could not be awarded damages [as far as I know], that is, the proceedings were only about my landlord's injunctive proceedings. I'd have to file as a CLAIMANT afresh to recover damages under The Defective Premises Act 1972 for the above wrongs;

    d) Note the use of dated newspapers. Since then, I have learnt how to activate the **date stamp** on my digital camera! If you're not sure what I mean, I have added a date stamp to the back cover of this book. Such a small detail can provide you with substantiated evidence. These days, everyone uses a smart phone, however as far as I know, it does not yet have a date stamp feature yet.

Judge's reaction Page 3:

1. I am not sure that the judge read my SKELETON ARGUMENT or looked at the diagram before the trial.

Page 4 of CASE 2, SKELETON ARGUMENT, the original, badly done

THE CLAIMANT'S APPLICATION DATED 25.2.2013 & SERVED 6.3.2013

My Social Landlord's N16A Application requests that I, the Defendant, must:

(1) Forthwith provide full unhindered access to the Claimant, its servants or age[nts]... [or Flat 5 Vaughan] Rd, London E15... [s]caffolding to all elevations of 5... and to remove the said scaffoldi[ng]... comprising the reroofing of th[e]... on pitched roofs and the taking... hand flank wall at roof level t[o]... first floor level to the back additi[on]...

Unnecessary to type out and use up valuable space in what should be a 3-page document. File copy of N16A at the back

Page **45**

However, the Application should be refused on the following:

[A] Main issue: MY LANDLORD OWES ME A DUTY OF CARE

My Social Landlord will "*be removing the entire roof,*" Jennifer Marius, email 4.3.2013

Page **138, para 2**

and, "*take down the parapet wall on the flank elevation to the main building and back addition… the brick parapet walls will be removed down to a plumb-line,*" Jennifer Marius, email 13.2.2013.

However, I am to remain **in situ** while these works take place.

Page **113, point 3 & 4**

My Social Landlord wishes their building works to take place without any Duty of Care to me as their Assured Tenant despite knowledge of my injuries caused by building works. I refer to this later.

Tenancy Agreement **Tab 1**

Meanwhile, Dr Chang writes in her medical report dated 22.4.2013:

"*it is my opinion that the proposed building works will probably affect Miss Christian's health, where the stress will probably exacerbate her anxiety, Post traumatic Stress Disorder, and Systemic Lupus Erythematosus.*"

Page **261**

Some photographs of my previous injuries caused by building works on same Premises.

Page **64 - 65**

Comment on Page 4:

1. I did not need to put point (1) in the argument. Underline important text with a <u>red</u> pen and ruler;

2. The main issue was Duty of Care;

3. The GP medical report was an excellent idea but cost me £50 while my weekly income was £50. [It's quite stressful getting a relevant medical report—surgery staff can be incompetent.]

Judge's reaction Page 4:

1. Judges, in my limited experience, seem to automatically believe that organizations are telling the truth in court, so you, the LIP, must ask why there is an absence of obvious evidence such as a surveyor's report—The judge was not acquainted with the building profession;

2. The judge interrupted to say that I was "*not helping*" my case. Intimidating, to say the least. I should have asked the judge what she meant;

3. After the second interruption, I held my ground and the judge replied dryly: "*We have moved on from that.*" I should have asked the judge what she meant by this;

Page 5 of CASE 2, SKELETON ARGUMENT, the original, badly done

Points of Law

My Landlord owes me a Duty of Care in common law and or in:

The Defective Premises Act 1972
4 Landlord's duty of care in virtue of obligation or right to repair premises demised
(1) Where premises are let under a tenancy which puts on the landlord an obligation to the tenant for the maintenance or repa... ...rsons who might reasonably be expected to be affec... ...duty to take such care as is reasonable in all the circ... ...afe from personal injury or from damage to their prop...

Unnecessary to type out and use up valuable space. File copy of legislation at the back

Submissions of fact

1) Mrs Christine Connolly of 5A Vaughan Rd was rehoused on 11.2.2013, but I was not.

2) I have emailed my Landlord my medical information 12 times from 3.10.2011 to 19.2.2013, as shown in my Particulars from Page **172 - 183**, & with the Exhibits: A,B,C,D

Exhibits on Page **66 – 74**, Exhibit G Page **128** Systemic Lupus

[Pages **278 – 282** read pgs **29, 30** missing in Witness Statement], & **71**

Summary

If the Landlord carries out its tardy, invasive works, outstanding since the Council's Notice on Dangerous Structures for repair within 24 hours and dated 30.9.2011... and I am in situ: foreseeable Negligence will take place, & my health will be ruined.

Exhibit F Page **65**

The Landlord has a motive to incapacitate me, which I explain under **Issue D**.
That is why they have not accepted my **Draft Undertaking*** of 26.3.2013, nor my Amended Undertaking* of 14.6.2013 to be rehoused.

Tab 2

Comment on Page 5:

1. It is best to only mention the relevant point and file a copy of the legislation at the back. You need to save a much space as possible within your SKELETON ARGUMENT;

2. Page 5 could have been merged with page 4, but it's hard to see the wood for the trees…

Judge's reaction Page 5:

1. The judge asked the barrister if I was living in a multi-storey building or an ordinary house. I don't think the barrister understood the implication of the question;

2. I feel that the Submission of Fact added weight to the judge's decision to award my landlord no costs. This is reflected in the transcript of the judge's judgment, for which I had to borrow £140 to purchase;

Page 6 of CASE 2, SKELETON ARGUMENT, the original, badly done

[B.1] Issue: FREQUENCY OF ACCESS

Point (1) of the Claimant's N16A Application on page 45 requests: `"full unhindered access… to erect … and to remove the said scaffolding…"`

The Application omits the words '*access is only required 2 times*', but Jennifer Marius confirms in her email of 8.2.2013: "*access is only required on two occasions*", as does Mrs Bennett at both court hearings.

However, this is completely untrue.

Page 105, para 2

Submissions of fact

1) **Point 3**: "*… Unfortunately because the scaffolding needs to [sic] erected to all elevations of the building until our contractors arrive on site they will not be able to determine how long this will take or how much scaffolding will be required*" — Thus indicating a need for additional access, while no project management inspection has taken place.

2) **Point 3, para 2**: "*… however, should additional access be required to complete the foundation of the scaffolding… ensure you are informed*" — Thus indicating potential need for more access.

Jennifer Marius, email 13.2.2013   Page **112**

1) **Para 2**: "*My understanding is that should the alarm be triggered a message will be transmitted automatically to the contractor who will attend to investigate the cause.*" — Thus indicating additional need for access & my communication with the contractor at whatever hour of the day or night, and with no thought for my need to contact the police.

Jennifer Marius, email 15.2.2013 **at 17.15hrs**   Page **121**

1) **Point 1**: "*I am unable to give you an exact time that the contractor will begin to erect the scaffolding in Faraday Road because the operatives will first need to attend the site to determine what the job entails.*" — Faraday Road is a public road with no access issues preventing job determination, indicating no ability to pre-plan.

2) **Point 4**: "*may take longer than one day to [sic] for them to complete*" — Thus indicating more need for access.

Jennifer Marius, email 18.2.2013   Page **126**

Comment on Page 6:

1. This page was inspired by District Judge Murch's question on the landlord's application that access was only required on "*two occasions*". I may have shot myself in the foot with this one;

2. N16A—that's the form you use if you wish to try to take out an injunction against someone.

Judge's reaction Page 6:

1. The district judge had said I was "*not helping my case*". I replied that another judge had asked me if I could prove if "*more than 2 occasions of access were required by my landlord*". The judge allowed me to continue;

2. After judgment was passed, the judge said to the barrister, who was to write up the Court Order, that she would help the barrister in the wording of the Order, and that the barrister should not write "*two occasions of access or eight weeks*", thereby allowing the works to potentially continue indefinitely. My heart sank;

3. Indeed, you will see in the final Court Order that there was no mention of access or duration at all. In fact, <u>no essential works were ever done</u> while I lived there, that is, the DANGEROUS STRUCTURE continued to exist above my front door for another 2 years <u>after the trial;</u>

4. The structure could have collapsed and injured any person.

Page 7 of CASE 2, SKELETON ARGUMENT, the original, badly done

1) **Middle of Para 4:** "*I can also confirm that we do propose to take photographs of your garden before and after the works are completed to ensure...*" — Thus indicating 2 more needs for access.

Jennifer Marius, email 1.3.2013   Page **133**

Summary

My Landlord's Application of 2 needs of access does not hold true.

****

[B.2] Issue: "UNHINDERED ACCESS"

The Claimant's N16A Application on page 45 asks the Defendant to:
(2) Give to the Claimant, its servants or agents full unhindered access to the Premises, at all reasonable hours of the daytime to inspect and carry out repairs to the Premises or the building upon being provided with 24 hours notice.

However, if the Landlord only requires 2 occasions of access, why do they want full unhindered access to the Premises without limitation?

Submissions of fact

1) My self-employed working week does not take place at home, unless I am ill, so I cannot provide full unhindered access to the Premises. While a recent investigation by the Inland Revenue into my self-employment places a strain on me to maintain my work ethic.

Inland Revenue Page **141 para 3, 139**

2) If I am offered ESOL teaching again this summer then I need to leave the house prior to 7.00am. If I do not attend, I will lose the work and it may not be offered again.

Summary

I am entitled to try to earn a living in my self-employment without incessant interruption as happened over the last 8 years. My self employment is not at home.

My legal advisor on Inland Revenue Page **122**

7

Comment on Page 7:

> 1. This page was about Frequency of Access and highlighted a lack of consistency shown by the landlord's legal representative.
>
> I could have managed without this page.

Judge's reaction Page 7:

> 1. However, on the day, I felt as though the judge *was* listening to the difficulties I experienced over many years created by my landlord in relation to my self-employment as seen on the page.

Page 8 of CASE 2, SKELETON ARGUMENT, the original, badly done

[B.3] Issue: DURATION OF WORKS

Jennifer Marius refers to the Landlord's proposed works as taking 6 - 8 weeks.

Page **105**, para 3

Submissions of fact

1) *GallifordTry Partnership* Ltd --- the Landlord's associate --- did trespass, damage, occupy my garden & injure me, while the Landlord turned a blind eye, in what was meant to be 8 weeks, but which lasted from 5.6.2005 to 21.8.2006, more than a year.

    I litigated and settled in a Minute of Order. The compensation went on my losses.

Page **60 - 63**

2) From February 2009 to 5 April 2012, my Landlord took more than 2 years to do a gutter repair, & required incessant access from me, causing distress and detracting from my recuperation. The full horror of this is documented in my irrefutable Particulars.
    However, my own contractor fixed the 2-year gutter problem in 45 minutes in July 2012.

My particulars Page, **143 - 184**

    My Witness Statement gives a photographic account with dated newspapers.

Under Defendant's Evidence **273 - 278**

    Landlord's roof reports: 11.5.2009, 29.11.2010, & my contractor's receipt July 2012.

Tab 4

3) On 7.10.2011, Police CAD ref: 4436 / Diagram B: my Landlord demolished my garden wall instead of the Dangerous Structure over my door, & has never been rebuilt it in 20 months, exposing me to trespassers.

You need missing pages of my Witness Statement Page **282 – 284**, page **75**

Points of Law

Civil law is based on probability.
[Point 3] was a breach of the Landlord & Tenant Act 1985, Section 11, *Repairing obligations* --- no written notice 24 hours in advance, was followed by Trespass to the Land as shown by photos in Diagram B.]

Summary

It is highly probable based on the above that the proposed works will not take 6 - 8 weeks but will exceed a year, endangering my health and ruining my income. At 55 years of age, I have already had the last 8 years of my life ruined by the Landlord, and it would be nice to regain my Quiet Enjoyment before I become a penniless pensioner.

Comment on Page 8:

1. This page was probably unnecessary except for para 2) plus the evidence filed at the back;

2. While it is compelling that the landlord demolished the wrong wall, it all becomes too much for the judge to take on board;

Judge's reaction Page 8:

1. In the court transcript, the judge referred to my being undermined by my landlord, but she did not ensure in her Judgment or final Court Order that I would not be further undermined by the landlord. For example, dates in relation to the <u>duration</u> of building works were <u>not</u> included, that is, she did not confine the building works to a time limit as you'd expect in an injunction application / undertaking;

3. A Pro bono solicitor later told me that the Order should have contained time limits as it was an Injunction Order, and that the landlord should have adhered to its own undertaking. It is very strange that no dates were put into the Order and a year or more later, nothing was done.

Page 9 of CASE 2, SKELETON ARGUMENT, the original, badly done

[C] Issue: TEMPORARY ACCOMMODATION

Point of Law

1) My Tenancy Agreement states: **Temporary vacation of Premises** (16) Where the Association is required to, or deems it necessary to carry out repairs or other works [...] reasonably be carried out whilst [...] ation of the Premises then:-

    (a) In exchange for th[...] ernative and temporary accommodation [...] Premises for as long as it is necess[ary...]

    (b) Upon the works bein[g...] of which the Association's decision shall be final) the tenant shall vacate the temporary accommodation and reoccupy the Premises;

[overlay note: Repetitious, and should have been filed at the back with other legislation anyway]

Tab 1 see pg 9

However, Jennifer Marius did not refer to temporary rehousing until her email of 25.2.2013, the same day she filed these N16A proceedings --- an act of aggression.
Page **129**

The proposed Marlin Apartments it is not suitable because:

Submissions of Fact

1) **Para 4**: "*these are serviced apartment you will not have neighbours per se as the apartments are generally occupied by corporate organisations*" — If the proposed works continue for a year or more, this will be extremely unpleasant for me
Jennifer Marius email 1.3.2013   Page **133**

2) **Para 3**: "*...Marlin Apartments they have advised that they will not be able to accommodate your cat there... cattery located in Leyton...*" — If my elderly cat is put in a cattery for 8 weeks to a year, this will finish him off, while my Landlord is happy to spend between £600 [for 8 weeks] to £3,900 [a year] on a cattery. The Leyton cattery refer in their email to distress to the cat.
Jennifer Marius email 4.3.2013: Page **138**, Cattery Page **285**, vet opinion *tba*

3) Mrs Connelly has been in Marlin Apartments since 11.2.2013 because my Social Landlord put her there, while they have been happy to let her have damp walls in 5A Vaughan Road for some years
Page **179**, Particular 305

9

Comment on Page 9:

1. I did not need to repeat the point of law of my tenancy agreement;

2. The first section is scrubbed out, because that was better left for when the witness was being cross-examined by myself;

3. The second section is scrubbed out, because it is not a significant point to have within a short 3-page document;

4. The third section is scrubbed out, because it is not a significant point;

5. The section remaining was significant, because the temporary accommodation would not house my elderly cat;

6. Was this page necessary? 2) Para 3 was the only part worth having in the argument.

Judge's reaction Page 9:

1. In fact, the judge took an interest in the vet's report presented on the day, although the transcript of the trial showed that the judge reduced the cat's medical conditions to being "*a little deaf*", whereas he was arthritic, had kidney disease and thyroid disease—pills were needed daily—and lastly, he was profoundly deaf not "a little deaf".

Page 10 CASE 2, SKELETON ARGUMENT, the original, badly done

Summary

My Amended Undertaking* to be rehoused presents better value for money and safeguards my health and that of my pet. G15 is a group of housing providers enabling a change in housing provider.

Tab 3

[D] Issue: MY LANDLORD HAS BAD INTENTIONS TOWARDS ME

My Social Landlord has bad intentions towards me because:

i. They turned a blind eye during the illegal occupation of my garden by *Gallifordtry Partnerships Ltd*, their associate, and I ranted about this bitterly by email and letter;

ii. They provided a fake Party Wall Award document to *Gallifordtry Partnerships Ltd* which was *Gallifordtry's* only defence document and resulted in 2 years of Bow County Court's wasted time, and was an attempt to pervert the course of justice. I ranted about this bitterly by email and letter;

iii. I have an outstanding claim for the Landlord's 100[s] of breaches of my tenancy agreement, disrepair and trespass;

iv. I dared to lodge a complaint about Elaine Marshall to the SRA;

Page **110 - 111**

Submissions of fact

1) Throughout 2012, I sought mediation with *LawWorks* but Elaine Marshall lied to them, as proven by my court transcript [wherein my attempt to get an interim injunction against the Landlord was mal-administered by the court, no costs to me] dated 20.1.2012

Page **78 – 79**, Transcript **82 - 83**

2) On 10.11.2012 in fear of my Landlord, Safer Neighbourhood Police opened a file with crime ref: **KTRT 0040 653**. On 13.6.2013, DJ Murcher refused me permission to file this.

3) I sought mediation with the Landlord's own mediator *Common Ground*, but the Director refused, and suggested I contact Samaritans.

Tab 3 Page maybe **286b**

4) The Landlord removed me from www.homeswapper.co.uk

Tab 3 Page maybe **286d – 286e**

10

Comment on Page 10:

1. I would rephrase or remove the opening paragraph now;

2. The first section is scrubbed out, because while significant, the point was not specific to the proposed building works;

3. The second section is scrubbed out, because it is of lesser significance;

4. The only section worth retaining is the point about the landlord removing me from www.homeswapper.co.uk. While you would think they would hope to get rid of me, in fact, they removed me from the website, because my uploaded photos representing 5 Vaughan Road showed its reality—back garden flooded with raw sewage, my cellulitis infection, damp interior walls, and so on.

Judge's reaction Page 10:

1. I was able to show the judge high resolution images in place of the deliberately badly photocopied images in the trial bundle;

2. The judge summarized all matters in her judgment and said that my landlord had <u>not</u> listened to me. This contributed to the landlord losing their legal costs.

Page 11 CASE 2, SKELETON ARGUMENT, the original, badly done

Summary

The Landlord wishes to incapacitate me with distressing, dangerous & invasive building works because:

-- The Landlord attempted to pervert the course of justice in *Christian v Gallifordtry*, wasting 2 years of Bow County Court's time, and I ranted about it by email.

-- I have an my outstanding claim. See what maybe page 286A under **Tab 3**.

This is shown by the fact they have refused to mediate throughout 2012.

The Landlord Application requires more than 2 occasions of access, and works will probably go on for more than a year -- not 6 to 8 weeks.

Marlin Apartments is unsuitable temporary and or long-term housing, & my cat will probably die in the cattery.

I remain in fear of the Landlord.

The Undertaking*:

My Amended Undertaking*, last page within **Tab 2**, removes all obstacles.

Skeleton Argument prepared by Ms Yolanda Christian acting as a litigant-in-person

Dated this   Monday   day of   1 5 July 2013

Signed

Miscellaneous

On 18.7.2013, the district judge asked us to leave the courtroom while she decided on her judgment. What was going to happen? If my landlord was to be allowed to remove the roof and walls around me, I knew I'd become ill, and that my then medical conditions would be exacerbated. In addition, falling slates, or whatever, could have injured my cat, and he'd already been previously injured on the Gallifordtry Try build. If I was to be forced to go to Marlin Apartments and my elderly sick cat was put into a cattery for 2 years, it would have been better to have him put down.

At some point during the trial, the judge asked us how far away Marlin Apartments was from my home. I answered with complete honesty: "*It is near*". However, if she had asked me—"*What problems would be presented to you if you were asked to commute daily from Marlin Apartments to your home in order to feed your cat and administer medication to it?*" then I would have responded with the same honesty, "*ongoing severe fatigue would make that difficult, and while also struggling with my self-employment*".

The judge had already heard from me that I felt the need to sleep every afternoon due to intense fatigue caused by the previous actions of the landlord's associate, Gallifordtry Partnerships Ltd, but she seemingly forgot this and decided that, because I had said the word "*near*" that I could commute daily between the two addresses. The transcript states that I said it was "*very near*", but I do not remember saying "*very*". I did not say it. [In any transcript request, the judge gets to approve it and make amendments before it is issued to the purchaser.]

The Judge went on to order that my landlord, East Thames Group Ltd:

- Fix my hot water;

- Provide me with a decant policy;

- Put me up in Marlin Apartments;

- Provide me with a Schedule of Works;

- Provide me with 7-days' notice before work began;

- Leave the cat to stay on the Premises. I was to go back to feed it daily, however this wording did not make it into the Court Order;

- Liaise with me as to how the actual decant took place, i.e. removal van or taxi.

The Court Order follows

The final Court Order in Case 2

Injunction Order
Between Yolanda Christian, Defendant
And East Thames Group [sic 'Ltd' missed off], **Claimant**
In the Bow County Court
Claim Number 3BO00662

If you do not obey this Order you will be guilty of contempt of court and you may be sent to prison.

Before DISTRICT JUDGE DAVIES on 18 July 2013 the court considered an application for an injunction UPON hearing Counsel for the Claimant & the Defendant in person.

AND UPON the Claimant agreeing to accommodate the Defendant in Marlin Apartments, Bellhaven, 2 Millstone Close, Windmill Lane, London E15 1PE ("Marlin Apartments") until the completion of the repair works in the attached Schedule [1] & to provide by way of assistance to facilitate the move from Ground Floor Flat, 5 Vaughan Rd, London E15 4AA ("the premises").

AND UPON the Claimant agreeing to provide its decant policy within 7 days [2] & to undertake any necessary works to the hot water system [3], the garden wall [4] & the tree in the garden of the premises [5] during the Defendant's absence from the premises in Marlin Apartments [6].

The Court ordered that Yolanda Christian

1. The Defendant must forthwith provide full unhindered access to the Claimant [7], its servants or agents to the garden of ground Floor Flat, 5 Vaughan Rd, London E15 4AA ("the premises") to erect scaffolding to all elevations of 5 Vaughan Road ("the building") & to remove the said scaffolding after completion of works comprising the re-roofing of the main building & back addition pitched roofs & take down & rebuilding of the right hand flank wall at roof level to the main building & at first floor level to the back additions at 5a Vaughan Road.

2. The Defendant must give to the Claimant, its servants and agents full unhindered access to the premises at all reasonable hours of the daytime to inspect & carry out repairs to the premises or the building upon being provide with 24 hours' notice. [8]

This Order shall remain in force until the completion of the works unless before then it is revoked by further order of the court. [9]

It is further ordered that

There be no Order as to costs. [10]

Stuck on the second page of the Court Order was a one-line entry, which could easily have been overlooked:

"You are entitled to apply to the court to reconsider the Order before the day."

Analysis of the Court Order:

The judge had already indicated that the barrister would write up the Court Order with her assistance, however:

– **attached Schedule** [1]

The Schedule was <u>not</u> attached to the Court Order posted to me and was never provided. That is, the court posted the Court Order to me without querying the absence of the Schedule. The court then refused to do anything about the absence, and while the barrister also did nothing about it and while she had apparently written up the Court Order.

– **provide its decant policy within 7 days** [2]

The decant policy *was* sent to me quickly by email. It's strange as to why the landlord would not provide it to me in the first place as my tenancy agreement gives me the right to ask for it, and they wanted me to decant the premises for the important building works.

Where the Order says, "*provide its decant policy within 7 days*", I feel that's a deliberate inaccuracy. The 7 days referred to the amount of Notice I was to be given when the building works were to begin, in order to give me time to decant. It was not to do with the issuing of the decant policy.

– **undertake any necessary works to hot water system** [3]

The district judge thoughtfully sought to reduce the amount of disruption I had been experiencing by enquiring about outstanding repairs to my Premises. I had spent many months without hot water and the landlord had repeatedly ignored my requests to repair it and while I was in court facing them. I had been boiling pans of water for a shallow bath throughout a hot summer and to wash dishes and do housework, while the landlord terrorized me during their legal proceedings, and while coping with my ongoing and vulnerable health. I am quite sure this was a deliberate act to inconvenience me to the maximum.

– the garden wall [4]

The district judge sought to reduce the amount of disruption to me by enquiring about other repairs. This refers to the landlord having demolished my substantial garden wall on 7 October 2011, instead of the Dangerous Structure above the front doors of 5 and 5a Vaughan road. The inappropriate demolition was carried out without notice and then they never rebuilt it. Meanwhile, neighbours held me responsible for the eyesore, which added to my distress. Despite the Court order, the repair of the garden wall was never done during my occupancy.

– and the tree in the garden of the premises [5]

The district judge sought to reduce the amount of future disruption to me by enquiring about other outstanding repairs. I had shown her a letter from the council in which the landlord had previously applied to the Council to pollard the protected Ash tree in my garden. In the absence of follow through by my landlord, the tree had grown substantially and might have caused damage to a neighbouring property.

– The Defendant must forthwith provide full unhindered access to the Claimant [7]

Why was this added if I was to be living in Marlin Apartments?

– provide with 24 hours' notice [8]

This was completely inappropriate as I was to receive 7 days' Notice for the decant to Marlin Apartments;

– unless before then it is revoked by further order of the court. [9]

How could I revoke the Court Order after all I had been through on my own? I had lost 11 pounds in weight. I was impoverished and ill. My hair was falling out.

– There be no Order as to costs. [10]

The district judge showed the landlord what she thought of them by not allowing them any of their £8,500 legal costs. And according to Jennifer Marius, witness and area manager for the landlord, [who spoke freely *throughout* the whole trial], there was an additional loss of £11,000 in having put the upstairs tenant in Marlin Apartments while emails between us had ensued, and then the landlord's subsequent legal actions had taken place. Jennifer Marius gave me this information during the trial as she spoke at all times when she felt like it, which is not appropriate court protocol. Jennifer persisted in the belief that the expensive and draining fiasco was all my fault, when it was all her fault for not observing the law contained in my tenancy agreement. Further costs incurred were for their in-house solicitor.

I am sorry to tell you that the judge ignored my right as to Costs under The Litigants in Person (Costs & Expenses) Act 1975. I have a sneaky suspicion that such costs for the litigant-in-person are rarely considered.

I am sorry to tell you that after the trial and because the barrister did not write up the verbal order of the judge accurately, and because she chose to omit that the cat was <u>not</u> be put into a cattery but stay on the Premises—I was forced to purchase a court transcript at my own expense to dispute this with Jennifer Marius via a support worker. I am grateful to a friend for lending me the money for the transcript.

What happened in the end?

The building works didn't take place at 5 Vaughan Road and my Premises became noticeably damp. My possessions began to suffer from mildew. The landlord refused to provide modest financial assistance so that I could buy cleaning products or plastic crates to protect my things from dampness and the results of that dampness.

A charity came to the rescue and sent me plastic crates to pack some things, however my furniture had by now developed mildew and had to be disposed of—a very smart writing desk had to be gotten rid of, because the Premises were now consumed with mould mites—tiny white creatures everywhere, including my wardrobe and in my underwear drawer!

Internet research had informed me that the best way to deal with mould mites was to regularly vacuum, including vacuuming the walls, and that it was important to maintain a warm well-ventilated atmosphere. Vacuuming was easy enough to do, if not exhausting and using up electricity, and I was lucky enough to have an efficient German vacuum cleaner with nifty accessories. However, I had no control over the continuing dampness and couldn't afford to heat the Premises.

Jennifer Marius declared that she was willing to send me a contractor, *Pest Control*, although *Pest Control* had never dealt with mould mites before and while the Internet advised that there was no pest control solution, in terms of powders or sprays, and that vacuuming and good ventilation was the only solution. In the end, Jennifer Marius said she could not help me, because I had *refused* access to the contractor. This meant, yet again, I had to make the effort to reply that she had *not* offered me any appointment in the first place, so how could I have refused access to the contractor?

At least, I was with my cat and able to look after him. And thanks to organizations such as the PDSA and their free treatment for pets.

Finally, after exerting myself one last time—and it was a major effort to communicate with them in the local telephone kiosk—a well-known housing charity agreed to act as mediator, because I was in fear of my landlord. In September 2014 with the housing charity's support, I was able to leave the evil grasp of East Thames Group Ltd.

Meanwhile, they refused to pay me a Homeloss payment of £4,500, but paid me a Decant payment of £1,000 instead and laid on a van.

Crown Removals, hired by my landlord, damaged my favorite dining table despite thick padding [my thick duvet cover wrapped round it] and their best assurances of additional blankets being added.

The van hire men were unpleasant to me at first, probably on the advice of my landlord, but they soon warmed to me especially when I tipped them a round of beer. However, their other man, who arrived separately to install my washing machine and cooker, damaged the brand-new kitchen flooring and left abruptly without a goodbye. I felt he contrived this behavior on the instruction of my landlord.

In my new home, I was introduced to new problems—white paint was thrown down over me from a balcony above and while I was a total stranger to the "neighbour". The same person squirted bleach on my washing left in my garden. My garden was and is used as a constant ashtray by the flat immediately above me with deliberate attempts to cause burns and the tenants are especially inspired to behave this way since the Grenfell tragedy, and one Sunday afternoon while I was having a rare peaceful moment, an athletic intruder jumped over my garden door.

My cat was traumatized by the move in 2014 and too afraid to use the garden. He was really put out with me for removing him from his territory. He developed a tumour in his gums on top of his other ailments and had to be put down.

I'm now a self-employed writer, but my ability to earn has never picked up since the fateful day of 5th July 2005, when Gallifordtry Partnerships Ltd, and then my previous landlord, consecutively deprived me of my rights.

―――――――――――――――

7. The Litigants in Person (Costs & Expenses) Act 1975

This information is based on research, which may be out of date.

The legislation:

The definition of costs is found in the CIVIL PROCEDURE RULES and includes: fees, charges, disbursements, expenses, remuneration and reimbursements allowed to a LITIGANT-IN-PERSON.

The rate was £9.25 / hour. Now it is £18.00 / hour. On googling this matter, I found that some websites still referred to the £9.25 rate. The general rule is that the LIP does not get more than two thirds of what the opposing solicitor claims in total.

The awarding of legal costs:

If the parties fail to settle their dispute and it proceeds to trial, then the issue of COSTS will be determined by the court unless the parties agree on COSTS. Here are some possible outcomes:

— **"loser pays"**: the general rule is that the unsuccessful party will pay the costs of the successful party;

— **"two-way cost shifting"**: either party might be responsible for the other's expenses depending on the court's decision;

— **"one-way cost shifting"**: a situation in which only one party faces this risk of having to pay the other's expenses;

— **"follow the event principle"**: while a court may depart from this rule, any departure is usually in the way of depriving a successful party of costs, and not about awarding costs to an unsuccessful party.

Rule 44.3(1) of Civil Procedure Rules states the court has discretion:

- as to whether costs are payable by one party to another;

- the amount of those costs;

- when such costs are to be paid.

In deciding what order to make, the court must consider all the circumstances—the conduct of the parties, whether a party succeeded in all or part of his claim, and if any payment into court or admissible settlement offer is due.

The point of law:
The Civil Procedure (Amendment) Rules 2013: CPR 46.5 with effect from 1 April 2013:

Litigants-in-person

46.5.—(1) This rule applies where the court orders (whether by summary assessment or detailed assessment) that the costs of a litigant in person are to be paid by any other person.

(2) The costs allowed under this rule will not exceed, except in the case of a disbursement, two-thirds of the amount which would have been allowed if the litigant in person had been represented by a legal representative.

(3) The litigant in person shall be allowed—
(a) costs for the same categories of—

(i) work; and

(ii) disbursements,

which would have been allowed if the work had been done or the disbursements had been made by a legal representative on the litigant in person's behalf;

(b) the payments reasonably made by the litigant in person for legal services relating to the conduct of the proceedings; and

(c) the costs of obtaining expert assistance in assessing the costs claim.

(4) The amount of costs to be allowed to the litigant in person for any item of work claimed will be—

(a) where the litigant can prove financial loss, the amount that the litigant can prove to have been lost for time reasonably spent on doing the work; or

(b) where the litigant cannot prove financial loss, an amount for the time reasonably spent on doing the work at the rate set out in Practice Direction 46.

(5) A litigant who is allowed costs for attending at court to conduct the case is not entitled to a witness allowance in respect of such attendance in addition to those costs.

(6) For the purposes of this rule, a litigant in person includes (a) a company or other corporation which is acting without a legal representative; and

(b) any of the following, who acts in person (except where any such person is represented by a firm in which that person is a partner)—

(i) a barrister;

(ii) a solicitor;

(iii) a solicitor's employee;

(iv) a manager of a body recognised under section 9 of the Administration of Justice Act 1985 (a); or

(v) a person who, for the purposes of the 2007 Act(b), is an authorised person in relation to an activity which constitutes the conduct of litigation (within the meaning of that Act).

Practice Direction

Litigants in person: rule 46.5

3.1 In order to qualify as an expert for the purpose of rule 46.5(3)(c) (expert assistance in connection with assessing the claim for costs), the person in question must be a –

(a) barrister;

(b) solicitor;

(c) Fellow of the Institute of Legal Executives;

(d) Fellow of the Association of Costs Lawyers;

(e) law costs draftsman, a member of the Academy of Experts;

(f) law costs draftsman, a member of the Expert Witness Institute.

3.2   Where a self-represented litigant wishes to prove that the litigant has suffered financial loss, the litigant should produce to the court any written evidence relied on to support that claim, and serve a copy of that evidence on any party against whom the litigant seeks costs <u>at least 24 hours before the hearing</u> at which the question may be decided.

3.3   A self represented litigant who commences detailed assessment proceedings under rule 47.5 should serve copies of written evidence with notice of commencement.

3.4   The amount, which may be allowed to a self represented litigant under rule 45.39(5)(b) and rule 46.5(4)(b), is £18 / hour.

(a) 1985 c. 61. Section 9 was amended by the Courts and Legal Services Act 1990, section 125(3), (7), Schedules 18 and 20; the Access to Justice Act 1999 section 106, Schedule 15 Part II; S.I. 2000/1119 regulation 37(3), Schedule 4 paragraph 15; the Legal Services Act 2007, section 177, 210, Schedule 16, Part 2, paragraphs 80 and 81 and Schedule 23; S.I. 2001/1090, regulation 1, 9, Schedule 5 paragraph 12; S.I. 2011/1716 article 4.

(b) 2007 c.29.

8. Some conclusions & recommendations

The Litigant:

1. The LITIGANT-IN-PERSON **should not** attend a hearing without someone there to support him / her. For example, a PSU volunteer;

2. The LITIGANT-IN-PERSON **should** try to ensure that a competent note of hearing is taken;

3. The LITIGANT-IN-PERSON **should** take heed on filing and serving as set out in this book;

4. The LITIGANT-IN-PERSON **should** be prepared to consider paying for court transcripts and expect obstacle and delay by court staff in reply to the request;

5. The LITIGANT-IN-PERSON **should** speak up in court so that the court recording is clear. The LITIGANT-IN-PERSON **should** ask the other side to speak up if they are obscuring the volume of their voice.

The Witness:

1. The Witness **should never** be allowed to talk freely in a trial or court hearing whenever he / she feels like it, just because he / she has a barrister representing his / her powerful employer;

2. All witnesses **should** bring ID to prove their identity in a court hearing as a matter of form.

The barrister:

1. The barrister **should not** be allowed to write up the Court Order when in opposition to the LITIGANT-IN-PERSON. This **should** be done by the judge and without input from the barrister, otherwise it is another example of the LIPs unequal access to the court, and it is a temptation to the barrister to behave in a dishonourable way on behalf of for his / her client;

2. The barrister **should not** be allowed to have private access to the judge **unless** the LITIGANT-IN-PERSON is present as well—unless the court wishes to invite prejudice and more unequal access to the law;

3. The barrister **should** be asked to show ID to the court usher when entering the court and 'signing in'. I refer to how legal representatives may sign in under different names, which is inappropriate. For example, I believe the landlord's solicitor attended a hearing in 2012 opposite me, however the barrister from Hardwicke Chambers was listed by the court usher;

4. The barrister **should not** be allowed to invite her Witness to sit next to her throughout the trial, and then allow the Witness / her Client to talk freely throughout the trial, and as and when the Witness feels like it.

The Judge:

1. How is the first-time LITIGANT-IN-PERSON to know about the existence of the CASE SUMMARY and SKELETON ARGUMENT if the judge dispenses with pre-trial checklist as happened to me in *East Thames Group Ltd v Christian*?

    This is another example of unequal access to the law for the LITIGANT-IN-PERSON, even if the intention is meant to be helpful or save time, or if the judge assumed I wasn't up the task. It **should** be the duty of all judges to mention the importance of these documents to the LITIGANT-IN-PERSON, so that equal access to the law is enhanced.

The Court:

1. The court **should** provide a relevant leaflet on how to compile a TRIAL BUNDLE for the LITIGANT-IN-PERSON with visuals aids. But none exists. By not providing this, we have another an example of unequal access to the law for the LITIGANT-IN-PERSON;

2. A county court **should never** deprive the LITIGANT-IN-PERSON of a court transcript if the LITIGANT-IN-PERSON is willing to pay for it;

3. The court transcript system is out of date. For example, recordings could be picked up by voice recognition software, saving the court a huge amount of time. A print out should be readily available as matter of form, thereby cutting down on the mischief of any party and reducing waste of court time;

4. When the LITIGANT-IN-PERSON exposes SUBMISSIONS ON THE TRIAL BUNDLE, the judge **should** punish the dishonourable legal representative. Disallowing their costs is not enough. They should serve a spell in jail and it should go towards their dismissal or debarment;

5. In general, the judge **should** come down hard on any solicitor or barrister, who seeks **prejudice** against the beleaguered LIP. I refer to the landlord's representatives knowingly ignoring a Court Order for a case conference meeting to decide on the content of the trial bundle, and encouraging a district judge to accept a ready-made

[dishonourable] trial bundle, at which point it was apparent that the barrister had planted prejudice into the judge's head as he treated me as the vexatious litigant;

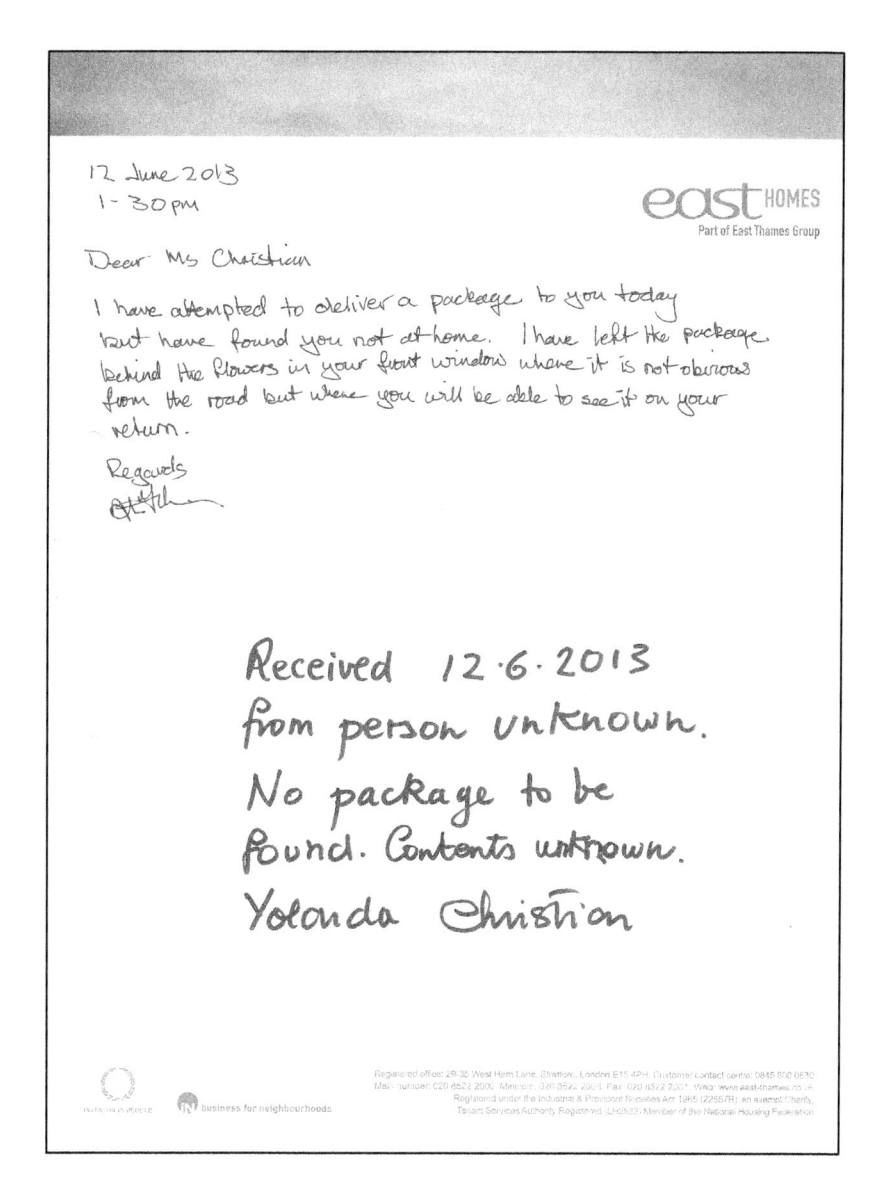

> 12 June 2013
> 1-30 pm
>
> **east** HOMES
> Part of East Thames Group
>
> Dear Ms Christian
>
> I have attempted to deliver a package to you today but have found you not at home. I have left the package behind the flowers in your front window where it is not obvious from the road but where you will be able to see it on your return.
>
> Regards
>
> Received 12.6.2013 from person unknown. No package to be found. Contents unknown.
> Yolanda Christian

The landlord had apparently left my copy of the trial bundle in my garden. Of course, it was not there.

This is unacceptable behaviour. It doesn't matter that the judge then tried to rectify the matter by setting the trial for a whole day so that I "*would have my say*", because:

- I had already been worn down by his aggressive attitude towards me on that day, and while I was clearly of vulnerable health as I sat there choking;

- He had already subjected me to unequal access to the law that day;

- I had already been usurped of my rights on the contents of the trial bundle, which later led to a lot of work for me regarding my preparation of SUBMISSIONS OF THE TRIAL BUNDLE;

- I had already been spoken to in a derisory way by the judge. This was intimidating and meant I had to be brave—**yet again**—and hold my ground, which made me feel ill afterwards;

- No judge **should** walk into court laden with prejudice towards the LITIGANT-IN-PERSON due to a barrister's antics;

6. The court **should** take responsibility when the company and or organization in opposition to the LITIGANT-IN-PERSON **fails** to comply with a final Court Order. It is not fair to expect the LITIGANT-IN-PERSON to do this.

9. SUMMARY OF CONCLUSIONS:

- There is no equal access to the law for the LITIGANT-IN-PERSON;

- The CASE SUMMARY and SKELETON ARGUMENT are vital for the LITIGANT-IN-PERSON to enhance the possibility of success;

- The CIVIL PROCEDURE RULES should be reformed;

- County courts would save time, money and energy if they allotted unusual cases, such as my Case 1 and Case 2, to the **same** judge, which would in turn reduce the shenanigans of the opposing legal representatives.

Printed in Great Britain
by Amazon